Unfolding Grace

FOR KIDS

Unfolding Grace for Kids: A 40-Day Journey through the Bible

Printed in China
Published by Crossway
Wheaton, Illinois 60187, USA
crossway.org

Crossway is a not-for-profit publishing ministry that exists solely for the purpose of publishing the Good News of the Gospel and the Truth of God's Word, the Bible. A portion of the purchase price of every ESV Bible is donated to help support Bible distribution ministry around the world.

The ESV Bible is free online and on mobile devices everywhere worldwide, including a selection of free Bible resources, at esv.org.

RRDS   28   27   26   25   24   23   22   21
9   8   7   6   5   4   3   2   1

Contents

Apostles

Creed

Introduction

We all love great stories—especially because we are all part of one! The Bible is filled with many great stories, but they are all part of one big story, the true story of our world.

The beginning of the Bible shows us the world as it was supposed to be. The first human beings were Adam and Eve. They lived in a happy and peaceful relationship with God, with each other, and with creation. Everything was very good in this place called Eden. But Adam and Eve disobeyed God, and now the world is filled with sin and sadness. Even so, God loves us and has a plan to forgive all who trust him and to fix everything that is broken. This is why Jesus came: to save sinners like us. Jesus lived a perfect life, died on the cross for our sins, rose again as our King, and sent his Spirit to be with us. He is now in heaven as our great Friend, and he will one day return to make everything very good again. Anyone who trusts Jesus will be forgiven so that God's people can know him, become like him, and live together in a new creation forever.

This is the big story of the Bible. It is the true story of this world. And it is a story of God's grace and kindness to us.

The purpose of *Unfolding Grace for Kids* is to lead us through the big story of the Bible. *Unfolding Grace for Kids* guides us with forty Bible readings. Each reading includes a short introduction to help us see the big picture of God's plan of grace. The biggest goal is to help us know the Author of this great story by seeing how he saves us. We learn that he is a Trinity—Father, Son, and Spirit—and is like a fountain that overflows with grace and love for sinners like us.

After reading *Unfolding Grace for Kids*, you will be ready to read the whole Bible with a sense of how it tells one big story of God's unfolding grace.

Part 1

THE STORY
BEGINS

God's Creation
and Humanity's Fall

The Bible's first words tell us about the beginning of the world. We learn how God creates everything and makes humans in his image. We learn how he makes us to enjoy his presence and to rule over his world. We learn that originally there was no sin, suffering, or sadness—everything was "very good."

But this story also shows the fall of mankind into sin. As a result of Adam and Eve's rejection of God, the world is now filled with sin, suffering, and death. Life is not the way it is supposed to be. Yet God graciously promises that a Savior will come to conquer Satan. This shows us that God will one day remove sin and death. He will restore his people to enjoy his presence and to rule the world again. God unfolds this gracious plan across the rest of the Bible.

GENESIS 1:1–31

In the beginning, God created the heavens and the earth. The earth was without form and void, and darkness was over the face of the deep. And the Spirit of God was hovering over the face of the waters.

And God said, "Let there be light," and there was light. And God saw that the light was good. And God separated the light from the darkness. God called the light Day, and the darkness he called Night. And there was evening and there was morning, the first day.

And God said, "Let there be an expanse in the midst of the waters, and let it separate the waters from the waters." And God made the expanse and separated the waters that were under the expanse from the waters that were above the expanse. And it was so. And God called the expanse Heaven. And there was evening and there was morning, the second day.

And God said, "Let the waters under the heavens be gathered together into one place, and let the dry land appear." And it was so. God called the dry land Earth, and the waters that were gathered together he called Seas. And God saw that it was good.

And God said, "Let the earth sprout vegetation, plants yielding seed, and fruit trees bearing fruit in which is their seed, each according to its kind, on the earth." And it was so. The earth brought forth vegetation, plants yielding seed according to their own kinds, and trees bearing fruit in which is their seed, each according to its kind. And God saw that it was good. And there was evening and there was morning, the third day.

And God said, "Let there be lights in the expanse of the heavens to separate the day from the night. And let them be for signs and for seasons, and for days and years, and let them be lights in the expanse of the heavens to give light upon the earth." And it was so. And God made the two great lights—the greater light to rule the day and the lesser light to rule the night—and the stars. And God set them in the expanse of the heavens to give light on the earth, to rule over the day and over the night, and to separate the light from the darkness. And God saw that it was good. And there was evening and there was morning, the fourth day.

And God said, "Let the waters swarm with swarms of living creatures, and let birds fly above the earth across the expanse of the heavens." So God created the great sea creatures and every living creature that moves, with which the waters swarm, according to their kinds, and every winged bird according to its kind. And God saw that it was good. And God blessed them, saying, "Be fruitful and multiply and fill the waters in the seas, and let birds multiply on the earth." And there was evening and there was morning, the fifth day.

And God said, "Let the earth bring forth living creatures according to their kinds—livestock and creeping things and beasts of the earth according to their kinds." And it was so. And God made the beasts of the earth according to their kinds and the livestock according to their kinds, and everything that creeps on the ground according to its kind. And God saw that it was good.

Then God said, "Let us make man in our image, after our likeness. And let them have dominion over the fish of the sea and over the birds of the heavens and over the livestock and over all the earth and over every creeping thing that creeps on the earth."

> So God created man in his own image,
>> in the image of God he created him;
>> male and female he created them.

And God blessed them. And God said to them, "Be fruitful and multiply and fill the earth and subdue it, and have dominion over the fish of the sea and over the birds of the heavens and over every living thing that moves on the earth." And God said, "Behold, I have given you every plant yielding seed that is on the face of all the earth, and every tree with seed in its fruit. You shall have them for food. And to every beast of the earth and to every bird of the heavens and to everything that creeps on the earth, everything that has the breath of life, I have given every green plant for food." And it was so. And God saw everything that he had made, and behold, it was very good. And there was evening and there was morning, the sixth day.

Now the serpent was more crafty than any other beast of the field that the LORD God had made.

He said to the woman, "Did God actually say, 'You shall not eat of any tree in the garden'?" And the woman said to the serpent, "We may eat of the fruit of the trees in the garden, but God said, 'You shall not eat of the fruit of the tree that is in the midst of the garden, neither shall you touch it, lest you die.'" But the serpent said to the woman, "You will not surely die. For God knows that when you eat of it your eyes will be opened, and you will be like God, knowing good and evil." So when the woman saw that the tree was good for food, and that it was a delight to the eyes, and that the tree was to be desired to make one wise, she took of its fruit and ate, and she also gave some to her husband who was with her, and he ate. Then the eyes of both were opened, and they knew that they were naked. And they sewed fig leaves together and made themselves loincloths.

And they heard the sound of the LORD God walking in the garden in the cool of the day, and the man and his wife hid themselves from the presence of the LORD God among the trees of the garden. But the LORD God called to the man and said to him, "Where are you?" And he said, "I heard the sound of you in the garden, and I was afraid, because I was naked, and I hid myself." He said, "Who told you that you were naked? Have you eaten of the tree of which I commanded you not to eat?" The man said, "The woman whom you gave to be with me, she gave me fruit of the tree, and I ate." Then the LORD God said to the woman, "What is this that you have done?" The woman said, "The serpent deceived me, and I ate."

The LORD God said to the serpent,

> "Because you have done this,
>> cursed are you above all livestock
>> and above all beasts of the field;
> on your belly you shall go,
>> and dust you shall eat
>> all the days of your life.
> I will put enmity between you and the woman,
>> and between your offspring and her offspring;
> he shall bruise your head,
>> and you shall bruise his heel."

The Flood and God's Covenant with Noah

Although God made everything good, people sinned and death spread to everyone. Over time people kept rejecting God and harming one another. Because of this, God judged the world by sending a flood. But God graciously allowed Noah, his family, and two of each animal to survive this flood. This shows us that although God is right to judge sinners, he also loves to show mercy.

After the flood God once again sent people into the world to be fruitful and multiply under his blessing. In his covenant (or special promise) with Noah, God promised never again to judge the world with a flood—and rainbows in the sky remind us of this promise. Instead, God would continue to unfold his gracious plan to send a Savior, give grace to sinners, and eventually renew all things.

In the six hundred and first year, in the first month, the first day of the month, the waters were dried from off the earth. And Noah removed the covering of the ark and looked, and behold, the face of the ground was dry. In the second month, on the twenty-seventh day of the month, the earth had dried out. Then God said to Noah, "Go out from the ark, you and your wife, and your sons and your sons' wives with you. Bring out with you every living thing that is with you of all flesh—birds and animals and every creeping thing that creeps on the earth—that they may swarm on the earth, and be fruitful and multiply on the earth." So Noah went out, and his sons and his wife and his sons' wives with him. Every beast, every creeping thing, and every bird, everything that moves on the earth, went out by families from the ark.

Then Noah built an altar to the LORD and took some of every clean animal and some of every clean bird and offered burnt offerings on the altar. And when the LORD smelled the pleasing aroma, the LORD said in his heart, "I will never again curse the ground because of man, for the intention of man's heart is evil from his youth. Neither will I ever again strike down every living creature as I have done. While the earth remains, seedtime and harvest, cold and heat, summer and winter, day and night, shall not cease."

And God blessed Noah and his sons and said to them, "Be fruitful and multiply and fill the earth. The fear of you and the dread of you shall be upon every beast of the earth and upon every bird of the heavens, upon everything that creeps on the ground and all the fish of the sea. Into your hand they are delivered. Every moving thing that lives shall be food for you. And as I gave you the green plants, I give you everything. But you shall not eat flesh with its life, that is, its blood. And for your lifeblood I will require a reckoning: from every beast I will require it and from man. From his fellow man I will require a reckoning for the life of man.

> "Whoever sheds the blood of man,
>   by man shall his blood be shed,
>   for God made man in his own image.

And you, be fruitful and multiply, increase greatly on the earth and multiply in it."

Then God said to Noah and to his sons with him, "Behold, I establish my covenant with you and your offspring after you, and with every living creature that is with you, the birds, the livestock, and every beast of the earth with you, as many as came out of the ark; it is for every beast of the earth. I establish my covenant with you, that never again shall all flesh be cut off by the waters of the flood, and never again shall there be a flood to destroy the earth." And God said, "This is the sign of the covenant that I make between me and you and every living creature that is with you, for all future generations: I have set my bow in the cloud, and it shall be a sign of the covenant between me and the earth. When I bring clouds over the earth and the bow is seen in the clouds, I will remember my covenant that is between me and you and every living creature of all flesh. And the waters shall never again become a flood to destroy all flesh. When the bow is in the clouds, I will see it and remember the everlasting covenant between God and every living creature of all flesh that is on the earth." God said to Noah, "This is the sign of the covenant that I have established between me and all flesh that is on the earth."

The sons of Noah who went forth from the ark were Shem, Ham, and Japheth. (Ham was the father of Canaan.) These three were the sons of Noah, and from these the people of the whole earth were dispersed.

Babel and the Promise to Abraham

God gave Noah and his family a fresh start. But it did not take long before humans again turned away from God. They built a great tower to show how great they were. But God interrupted their plans, confused their language, and scattered them over the earth.

But this raised questions. When would God send Eve's descendant—the Savior—who would defeat the Serpent and put an end to sin and death? How would God restore people to enjoy his presence like they did in Eden? We see God's plan unfold as he made a promise to Abraham. God promised him land, descendants, and blessing for all peoples. The Savior would come through Abraham.

GENESIS 11:1–9

Now the whole earth had one language and the same words. And as people migrated from the east, they found a plain in the land of Shinar and settled there. And they said to one another, "Come, let us make bricks, and burn them thoroughly." And they had brick for stone, and bitumen for mortar. Then they said, "Come, let us build ourselves a city and a tower with its top in the heavens, and let us make a name for ourselves, lest we be dispersed over the face of the whole earth." And the LORD came down to see the city and the tower, which the children of man had built. And the LORD said, "Behold, they are one people, and they have all one language, and this is only the beginning of what they will do. And nothing that they propose to do will now be impossible for them. Come, let us go down and there confuse their language, so that they may not understand one another's speech." So the LORD dispersed them from there over the face of all the earth, and they left off building the city. Therefore its name was called Babel, because there the LORD confused the language of all the earth. And from there the LORD dispersed them over the face of all the earth.

GENESIS 12:1–20

Now the Lord said to Abram, "Go from your country and your kindred and your father's house to the land that I will show you. And I will make of you a great nation, and I will bless you and make your name great, so that you will be a blessing. I will bless those who bless you, and him who dishonors you I will curse, and in you all the families of the earth shall be blessed."

So Abram went, as the Lord had told him, and Lot went with him. Abram was seventy-five years old when he departed from Haran. And Abram took Sarai his wife, and Lot his brother's son, and all their possessions that they had gathered, and the people that they had acquired in Haran, and they set out to go to the land of Canaan. When they came to the land of Canaan, Abram passed through the land to the place at Shechem, to the oak of Moreh. At that time the Canaanites were in the land. Then the Lord appeared to Abram and said, "To your offspring I will give this land." So he built there an altar to the Lord, who had appeared to him. From there he moved to the hill country on the east of Bethel and pitched his tent, with Bethel on the west and Ai on the east. And there he built an altar to the Lord and called upon the name of the Lord. And Abram journeyed on, still going toward the Negeb.

Now there was a famine in the land. So Abram went down to Egypt to sojourn there, for the famine was severe in the land. When he was about to enter Egypt, he said to Sarai his wife, "I know that you are a woman beautiful in appearance, and when the Egyptians see you, they will say, 'This is his wife.' Then they will kill me, but they will let you live. Say you are my sister, that it may go well with me because of you, and that my life may be spared for your sake." When Abram entered Egypt, the Egyptians saw that the woman was very beautiful. And when the princes of Pharaoh saw her, they praised her to Pharaoh. And the woman was taken into Pharaoh's house. And for her sake he dealt well with Abram; and he had sheep, oxen, male donkeys, male servants, female servants, female donkeys, and camels.

But the LORD afflicted Pharaoh and his house with great plagues because of Sarai, Abram's wife. So Pharaoh called Abram and said, "What is this you have done to me? Why did you not tell me that she was your wife? Why did you say, 'She is my sister,' so that I took her for my wife? Now then, here is your wife; take her, and go." And Pharaoh gave men orders concerning him, and they sent him away with his wife and all that he had.

Abraham and
the Promise of Isaac

Many years passed since God first promised to bless the world through Abraham's many descendants. But Abraham was now very old, and his wife, Sarah, could not have children. It did not look like God's plan could happen. Yet God still asked Abraham to trust him. He promised to give them a son, Isaac, and through him the blessing to all nations would come.

This chapter highlights a pattern in the Bible's story. God is a God who promises great things, and his people are those who trust him to do what he says. And when people trust him, he counts it to them as righteousness. As was Abraham, we are accepted not because of anything good we do but because of God's mercy and grace.

After these things the word of the LORD came to Abram in a vision: "Fear not, Abram, I am your shield; your reward shall be very great." But Abram said, "O Lord GOD, what will you give me, for I continue childless, and the heir of my house is Eliezer of Damascus?" And Abram said, "Behold, you have given me no offspring, and a member of my household will be my heir." And behold, the word of the LORD came to him: "This man shall not be your heir; your very own son shall be your heir." And he brought him outside and said, "Look toward heaven, and number the stars, if you are able to number them." Then he said to him, "So shall your offspring be." And he believed the LORD, and he counted it to him as righteousness.

And he said to him, "I am the LORD who brought you out from Ur of the Chaldeans to give you this land to possess." But he said, "O Lord GOD, how am I to know that I shall possess it?" He said to him, "Bring me a heifer three years old, a female goat three years old, a ram three years old, a turtledove, and a young pigeon." And he brought him all these, cut them in half, and laid each half over against the other. But he did not cut the birds in half. And when birds of prey came down on the carcasses, Abram drove them away.

As the sun was going down, a deep sleep fell on Abram. And behold, dreadful and great darkness fell upon him. Then the LORD said to Abram, "Know for certain that your offspring will be sojourners in a land that is not theirs and will be servants there, and they will be afflicted for four hundred years. But I will bring judgment on the nation that they serve, and afterward they shall come out with great possessions. As for you, you shall go to your fathers in peace; you shall be buried in a good old age. And they shall come back here in the fourth generation, for the iniquity of the Amorites is not yet complete."

When the sun had gone down and it was dark, behold, a smoking fire pot and a flaming torch passed between these pieces. On that day the LORD made a covenant with Abram, saying, "To your offspring I give this land, from the river of Egypt to the great river, the river Euphrates, the land of the Kenites, the Kenizzites, the Kadmonites, the Hittites, the Perizzites, the Rephaim, the Amorites, the Canaanites, the Girgashites and the Jebusites."

The Promise to Isaac
and the Blessing of Jacob

Early in the book of Genesis God promised to bless the world through Abraham's descendants. In story after story we see how God is faithful to this promise and how his people learn to trust him. For example, God was faithful to his promise to give Abraham a son—Isaac. And in response to God's faithfulness Abraham continually trusted him, even when it was hard.

In this next story we see how God passed along the promise to Abraham's son Isaac. God continues to pass along this promise from one generation to the next. No matter the obstacles, nothing will stand in God's way. He will bring his grace into our sinning and suffering world. A Savior will come through this family's line.

GENESIS 26:1–33

Now there was a famine in the land, besides the former famine that was in the days of Abraham. And Isaac went to Gerar to Abimelech king of the Philistines. And the LORD appeared to him and said, "Do not go down to Egypt; dwell in the land of which I shall tell you. Sojourn in this land, and I will be with you and will bless you, for to you and to your offspring I will give all these lands, and I will establish the oath that I swore to Abraham your father. I will multiply your offspring as the stars of heaven and will give to your offspring all these lands. And in your offspring all the nations of the earth shall be blessed, because Abraham obeyed my voice and kept my charge, my commandments, my statutes, and my laws."

So Isaac settled in Gerar. When the men of the place asked him about his wife, he said, "She is my sister," for he feared to say, "My wife," thinking, "lest the men of the place should kill me because of Rebekah," because she was attractive in appearance. When he had been there a long time, Abimelech king of the Philistines looked out of a window and saw Isaac laughing with Rebekah his wife. So Abimelech called Isaac and said, "Behold, she is your wife. How then could you say, 'She is my sister'?" Isaac said to him, "Because I thought, 'Lest I die because of her.'"

Abimelech said, "What is this you have done to us? One of the people might easily have lain with your wife, and you would have brought guilt upon us." So Abimelech warned all the people, saying, "Whoever touches this man or his wife shall surely be put to death."

And Isaac sowed in that land and reaped in the same year a hundredfold. The LORD blessed him, and the man became rich, and gained more and more until he became very wealthy. He had possessions of flocks and herds and many servants, so that the Philistines envied him. (Now the Philistines had stopped and filled with earth all the wells that his father's servants had dug in the days of Abraham his father.) And Abimelech said to Isaac, "Go away from us, for you are much mightier than we."

So Isaac departed from there and encamped in the Valley of Gerar and settled there. And Isaac dug again the wells of water that had been dug in the days of Abraham his father, which the Philistines had stopped after the death of Abraham. And he gave them the names that his father had given them. But when Isaac's servants dug in the valley and found there a well of spring water, the herdsmen of Gerar quarreled with Isaac's herdsmen, saying, "The water is ours." So he called the name of the well Esek, because they contended with him. Then they dug another well, and they quarreled over that also, so he called its name Sitnah. And he moved from there and dug another well, and they did not quarrel over it. So he called its name Rehoboth, saying, "For now the LORD has made room for us, and we shall be fruitful in the land."

From there he went up to Beersheba. And the LORD appeared to him the same night and said, "I am the God of Abraham your father. Fear not, for I am with you and will bless you and multiply your offspring for my servant Abraham's sake." So he built an altar there and called upon the name of the LORD and pitched his tent there. And there Isaac's servants dug a well.

When Abimelech went to him from Gerar with Ahuzzath his adviser and Phicol the commander of his army, Isaac said to them, "Why have you come to me, seeing that you hate me and have sent me away from you?" They said, "We see plainly that the LORD has been with you. So we said, let there be a sworn pact between us, between you and us, and let us make a covenant with you, that you will do us no harm, just as we have not touched you and have done to you nothing but good and have sent you away in peace. You are now the blessed of the LORD." So he made them a feast, and they ate and drank. In the morning they rose early and exchanged oaths. And Isaac sent them on their way, and they departed from him in peace. That same day Isaac's servants came and told him about the well that they had dug and said to him, "We have found water." He called it Shibah; therefore the name of the city is Beersheba to this day.

Israel Comes to Egypt

God's promises were gaining momentum. They passed from Abraham to Isaac and to Jacob, who had twelve sons (whose descendants would become the twelve tribes of Israel). Jacob had a favorite son—Joseph—and the other brothers came to resent Joseph for it. They sold him into slavery and told their father that he had died. Yet God was with Joseph, who was later sold in Egypt. God caused Joseph to rise to second-in-command over Egypt.

When a famine came upon the land of Canaan, Jacob's only hope was to send his remaining sons to Egypt for grain. When they arrived, they met Joseph again and learned an important lesson: God had been in control all along. God had planned for all of this to happen so that Joseph would be in a position to provide for them.

GENESIS 45:1–46:4

Then Joseph could not control himself before all those who stood by him. He cried, "Make everyone go out from me." So no one stayed with him when Joseph made himself known to his brothers. And he wept aloud, so that the Egyptians heard it, and the household of Pharaoh heard it. And Joseph said to his brothers, "I am Joseph! Is my father still alive?" But his brothers could not answer him, for they were dismayed at his presence.

So Joseph said to his brothers, "Come near to me, please." And they came near. And he said, "I am your brother, Joseph, whom you sold into Egypt. And now do not be distressed or angry with yourselves because you sold me here, for God sent me before you to preserve life. For the famine has been in the land these two years, and there are yet five years in which there will be neither plowing nor harvest. And God sent me before you to preserve for you a remnant on earth, and to keep alive for you many survivors. So it was not you who sent me here, but God. He has made me a father to Pharaoh, and lord of all his house and ruler over all the land of Egypt. Hurry and go up to my father and say to him, 'Thus says your son Joseph, God has made me lord of all Egypt. Come down to me; do not tarry. You shall dwell in the land of Goshen, and you shall be near me, you and your children and your children's children, and your flocks, your herds, and all that you have. There I will provide for you, for there are yet five years of famine to come, so that you and your household, and all that you have, do not come to poverty.' And now your eyes see, and the eyes of my brother Benjamin see, that it is my mouth that speaks to you. You must tell my father of all my honor in Egypt, and of all that you have seen. Hurry and bring my father down here." Then he fell upon his brother Benjamin's neck and wept, and Benjamin wept upon his neck. And he kissed all his brothers and wept upon them. After that his brothers talked with him.

When the report was heard in Pharaoh's house, "Joseph's brothers have come," it pleased Pharaoh and his servants. And Pharaoh said to Joseph, "Say to your brothers, 'Do this: load your beasts and go back to the land of Canaan, and take your father and your households, and come to me, and I will give you the best of the land of Egypt, and you shall eat the fat of the land.' And you, Joseph, are commanded to say, 'Do this: take wagons from the land of Egypt for your little ones and for your wives, and bring your father, and come. Have no concern for your goods, for the best of all the land of Egypt is yours.'"

The sons of Israel did so: and Joseph gave them wagons, according to the command of Pharaoh, and gave them provisions for the journey. To each and all of them he gave a change of clothes, but to Benjamin he gave three hundred shekels of silver and five changes of clothes. To his father he sent as follows: ten donkeys loaded with the good things of Egypt, and ten female donkeys loaded with grain, bread, and provision for his father on the journey. Then he sent his brothers away, and as they departed, he said to them, "Do not quarrel on the way."

So they went up out of Egypt and came to the land of Canaan to their father Jacob. And they told him, "Joseph is still alive, and he is ruler over all the land of Egypt." And his heart became numb, for he did not believe them. But when they told him all the words of Joseph, which he had said to them, and when he saw the wagons that Joseph had sent to carry him, the spirit of their father Jacob revived. And Israel said, "It is enough; Joseph my son is still alive. I will go and see him before I die."

So Israel took his journey with all that he had and came to Beersheba, and offered sacrifices to the God of his father Isaac. And God spoke to Israel in visions of the night and said, "Jacob, Jacob." And he said, "Here I am." Then he said, "I am God, the God of your father. Do not be afraid to go down to Egypt, for there I will make you into a great nation. I myself will go down with you to Egypt, and I will also bring you up again, and Joseph's hand shall close your eyes."

Part 2

GOD'S PEOPLE REDEEMED

Israel's Oppression
and Moses' Call

Genesis showed us the beginning of the Bible's story. We learned how God made the world good, how people's sin damaged it, and how God promised to send a Savior to restore his blessing. Then God advanced this promise with his covenant to Abraham: God promised to make Abraham a nation (Israel), to give that nation the land of Canaan, and to bless that nation so that it would be a blessing to all nations. It would be through Israel that God's Savior and blessing would come.

But Egypt's king eventually turned the Israelites into slaves. This makes us wonder: How would God fulfill these promises? We find the answer in the exodus story. We learn that as God worked to deliver Israel from slavery in Egypt, he was providing a picture of how he would one day send Jesus to rescue us from the deepest problems—the power of Satan, the grip of sin, and the punishment of death.

EXODUS 2:23–3:22

During those many days the king of Egypt died, and the people of Israel groaned because of their slavery and cried out for help. Their cry for rescue from slavery came up to God. And God heard their groaning, and God remembered his covenant with Abraham, with Isaac, and with Jacob. God saw the people of Israel—and God knew.

Now Moses was keeping the flock of his father-in-law, Jethro, the priest of Midian, and he led his flock to the west side of the wilderness and came to Horeb, the mountain of God. And the angel of the LORD appeared to him in a flame of fire out of the midst of a bush. He looked, and behold, the bush was burning, yet it was not consumed. And Moses said, "I will turn aside to see this great sight, why the bush is not burned." When the LORD saw that he turned aside to see, God called to him out of the bush, "Moses, Moses!" And he said, "Here I am." Then he said, "Do not come near; take your sandals off your feet, for the place on which you are standing is holy ground." And he said, "I am the God of your father, the God of Abraham, the God of Isaac, and the God of Jacob." And Moses hid his face, for he was afraid to look at God.

Then the LORD said, "I have surely seen the affliction of my people who are in Egypt and have heard their cry because of their taskmasters. I know their sufferings, and I have come down to deliver them out of the hand of the Egyptians and to bring them up out of that land to a good and broad land, a land flowing with milk and honey, to the place of the Canaanites, the Hittites, the Amorites, the Perizzites, the Hivites, and the Jebusites. And now, behold, the cry of the people of Israel has come to me, and I have also seen the oppression with which the Egyptians oppress them. Come, I will send you to Pharaoh that you may bring my people, the children of Israel, out of Egypt." But Moses said to God, "Who am I that I should go to Pharaoh and bring the children of Israel out of Egypt?" He said, "But I will be with you, and this shall be the sign for you, that I have sent you: when you have brought the people out of Egypt, you shall serve God on this mountain."

Then Moses said to God, "If I come to the people of Israel and say to them, 'The God of your fathers has sent me to you,' and they ask me, 'What is his name?' what shall I say to them?" God said to Moses, "I AM WHO I AM." And he said, "Say this to the people of Israel: 'I AM has sent me to you.'" God also said to Moses, "Say this to the people of Israel: 'The LORD, the God of your fathers, the God of Abraham, the God of Isaac, and the God of Jacob, has sent me to you.' This is my name forever, and thus I am to be remembered throughout all generations. Go and gather the elders of Israel together and say to them, 'The LORD, the God of your fathers, the God of Abraham, of Isaac, and of Jacob, has appeared to me, saying, "I have observed you and what has been done to you in

Egypt, and I promise that I will bring you up out of the affliction of Egypt to the land of the Canaanites, the Hittites, the Amorites, the Perizzites, the Hivites, and the Jebusites, a land flowing with milk and honey." ' And they will listen to your voice, and you and the elders of Israel shall go to the king of Egypt and say to him, 'The Lord, the God of the Hebrews, has met with us; and now, please let us go a three days' journey into the wilderness, that we may sacrifice to the Lord our God.' But I know that the king of Egypt will not let you go unless compelled by a mighty hand. So I will stretch out my hand and strike Egypt with all the wonders that I will do in it; after that he will let you go. And I will give this people favor in the sight of the Egyptians; and when you go, you shall not go empty, but each woman shall ask of her neighbor, and any woman who lives in her house, for silver and gold jewelry, and for clothing. You shall put them on your sons and on your daughters. So you shall plunder the Egyptians."

God's Judgment of Egypt

God began to deliver Israel from its slavery in Egypt. God decided to harden Pharaoh's heart so that he would not immediately let Israel go. Instead, God would judge Egypt with plagues before bringing Israel out.

Why did God do this? For this great reason: to teach Israel, Egypt, and the whole world that he alone is the one true God. He rules creation as a powerful God. He judges sin as a good God. And he saves his people as a gracious God. We see this in the stories of the plagues that God sent on Egypt, which begin in this section.

And the LORD said to Moses, "See, I have made you like God to Pharaoh, and your brother Aaron shall be your prophet. You shall speak all that I command you, and your brother Aaron shall tell Pharaoh to let the people of Israel go out of his land. But I will harden Pharaoh's heart, and though I multiply my signs and wonders in the land of Egypt, Pharaoh will not listen to you. Then I will lay my hand on Egypt and bring my hosts, my people the children of Israel, out of the land of Egypt by great acts of judgment. The Egyptians shall know that I am the LORD, when I stretch out my hand against Egypt and bring out the people of Israel from among them." Moses and Aaron did so; they did just as the LORD commanded them. Now Moses was eighty years old, and Aaron eighty-three years old, when they spoke to Pharaoh.

Then the LORD said to Moses and Aaron, "When Pharaoh says to you, 'Prove yourselves by working a miracle,' then you shall say to Aaron, 'Take your staff and cast it down before Pharaoh, that it may become a serpent.'" So Moses and Aaron went to Pharaoh and did just as the LORD commanded. Aaron cast down his staff before Pharaoh and his servants, and it became a serpent. Then Pharaoh summoned the wise men and the sorcerers, and they, the magicians of Egypt, also did the same by their secret arts.

For each man cast down his staff, and they became serpents. But Aaron's staff swallowed up their staffs. Still Pharaoh's heart was hardened, and he would not listen to them, as the LORD had said.

Then the LORD said to Moses, "Pharaoh's heart is hardened; he refuses to let the people go. Go to Pharaoh in the morning, as he is going out to the water. Stand on the bank of the Nile to meet him, and take in your hand the staff that turned into a serpent. And you shall say to him, 'The LORD, the God of the Hebrews, sent me to you, saying, "Let my people go, that they may serve me in the wilderness." But so far, you have not obeyed. Thus says the LORD, "By this you shall know that I am the LORD: behold, with the staff that is in my hand I will strike the water that is in the Nile, and it shall turn into blood. The fish in the Nile shall die, and the Nile will stink, and the Egyptians will grow weary of drinking water from the Nile." '" And the LORD said to Moses, "Say to Aaron, 'Take your staff and stretch out your hand over the waters of Egypt, over their rivers, their canals, and their ponds, and all their pools of water, so that they may become blood, and there shall be blood throughout all the land of Egypt, even in vessels of wood and in vessels of stone.' "

Moses and Aaron did as the LORD commanded. In the sight of Pharaoh and in the sight of his servants he lifted up the staff and struck the water in the Nile, and all the water in the Nile turned into blood. And the fish in the Nile died, and the Nile stank, so that the Egyptians could not drink water from the Nile. There was blood throughout all the land of Egypt. But the magicians of Egypt did the same by their secret arts. So Pharaoh's heart remained hardened, and he would not listen to them, as the LORD had said. Pharaoh turned and went into his house, and he did not take even this to heart. And all the Egyptians dug along the Nile for water to drink, for they could not drink the water of the Nile.

Seven full days passed after the LORD had struck the Nile.

God's Deliverance of Israel

The time finally came for God to deliver Israel from slavery. God judged Egypt with the death of its firstborn sons. But he spared Israel from this judgment. He told the Israelites to sacrifice a lamb and put its blood on their doorposts. If they did so, God's judgment would pass over their homes. This event pointed ahead to the greater deliverance that would come through Jesus. He was the Passover Lamb who was sacrificed on the cross so that God's judgment would pass over all who trust in him.

God then led Israel to the shore of the Red Sea. This next reading shows us what happened, and how God's people must trust the Lord alone to save.

EXODUS 14:1–31

T hen the LORD said to Moses, "Tell the people of Israel to turn back and encamp in front of Pi-hahiroth, between Migdol and the sea, in front of Baal-zephon; you shall encamp facing it, by the sea. For Pharaoh will say of the people of Israel, 'They are wandering in the land; the wilderness has shut them in.' And I will harden Pharaoh's heart, and he will pursue them, and I will get glory over Pharaoh and all his host, and the Egyptians shall know that I am the LORD." And they did so.

When the king of Egypt was told that the people had fled, the mind of Pharaoh and his servants was changed toward the people, and they said, "What is this we have done, that we have let Israel go from serving us?" So he made ready his chariot and took his army with him, and took six hundred chosen chariots and all the other chariots of Egypt with officers over all of them. And the LORD hardened the heart of Pharaoh king of Egypt, and he pursued the people of Israel while the people of Israel were going out defiantly. The Egyptians pursued them, all Pharaoh's horses and chariots and his horsemen and his army, and overtook them encamped at the sea, by Pi-hahiroth, in front of Baal-zephon.

When Pharaoh drew near, the people of Israel lifted up their eyes, and behold, the Egyptians were marching after them, and they feared greatly. And the people of Israel cried out to the LORD. They said to Moses, "Is it because there are no graves in Egypt that you have taken us away to die in the wilderness? What have you done to us in bringing us out of Egypt? Is not this what we said to you in Egypt: 'Leave us alone that we may serve the Egyptians'? For it would have been better for us to serve the Egyptians than to die in the wilderness." And Moses said to the people, "Fear not, stand firm, and see the salvation of the LORD, which he will work for you today. For the Egyptians whom you see today, you shall never see again. The LORD will fight for you, and you have only to be silent."

The LORD said to Moses, "Why do you cry to me? Tell the people of Israel to go forward. Lift up your staff, and stretch out your hand over the sea and divide it, that the people of Israel may go through the sea on dry ground. And I will harden the hearts of the Egyptians so that they shall go in after them, and I will get glory over Pharaoh and all his host, his chariots, and his horsemen. And the Egyptians shall know that I am the LORD, when I have gotten glory over Pharaoh, his chariots, and his horsemen."

Then the angel of God who was going before the host of Israel moved and went behind them, and the pillar of cloud moved from before them and stood behind them, coming between the host of Egypt and the host of Israel. And there was the cloud and the darkness. And it lit up the night without one coming near the other all night.

Then Moses stretched out his hand over the sea, and the Lord drove the sea back by a strong east wind all night and made the sea dry land, and the waters were divided. And the people of Israel went into the midst of the sea on dry ground, the waters being a wall to them on their right hand and on their left. The Egyptians pursued and went in after them into the midst of the sea, all Pharaoh's horses, his chariots, and his horsemen. And in the morning watch the Lord in the pillar of fire and of cloud looked down on the Egyptian forces and threw the Egyptian forces into a panic, clogging their chariot wheels so that they drove heavily. And the Egyptians said, "Let us flee from before Israel, for the Lord fights for them against the Egyptians."

Then the Lord said to Moses, "Stretch out your hand over the sea, that the water may come back upon the Egyptians, upon their chariots, and upon their horsemen." So Moses stretched out his hand over the sea, and the sea returned to its normal course when the morning appeared. And as the Egyptians fled into it, the Lord threw the Egyptians into the midst of the sea. The waters returned and covered the chariots and the horsemen; of all the host of Pharaoh that had followed them into the sea, not one of them remained. But the people of Israel walked on dry ground through the sea, the waters being a wall to them on their right hand and on their left.

Thus the Lord saved Israel that day from the hand of the Egyptians, and Israel saw the Egyptians dead on the seashore. Israel saw the great power that the Lord used against the

Egyptians, so the people feared the LORD, and they believed in the LORD and in his servant Moses.

God's Covenant with Israel

After God brought Israel out of slavery and across the sea, he led the people to Mount Sinai. It is here that they received God's commandments to learn how to live as his people. It is very good news that God did *not* say, "Obey my commands, and then I will rescue you from slavery." Instead, he said, "Now that I have saved you, I am going to show you how to respond with a life of love."

This is always how God works. He does not ask us to obey in order to earn salvation. Instead, he saves us by grace and then shows us how to respond with thankfulness and love. We will want to obey God only if we first know how much he loves us.

God's commands are also a gift. They show Israel how to live as a "kingdom of priests" in the world. This means that they are like a whole new humanity, like a new Adam. They are to show the world what it looks like to know God, love him, and treat others how he treats us.

On the third new moon after the people of Israel had gone out of the land of Egypt, on that day they came into the wilderness of Sinai. They set out from Rephidim and came into the wilderness of Sinai, and they encamped in the wilderness. There Israel encamped before the mountain, while Moses went up to God. The LORD called to him out of the mountain, saying, "Thus you shall say to the house of Jacob, and tell the people of Israel: 'You yourselves have seen what I did to the Egyptians, and how I bore you on eagles' wings and brought you to myself. Now therefore, if you will indeed obey my voice and keep my covenant, you shall be my treasured possession among all peoples, for all the earth is mine; and you shall be to me a kingdom of priests and a holy nation.' These are the words that you shall speak to the people of Israel."

So Moses came and called the elders of the people and set before them all these words that the LORD had commanded him. All the people answered together and said, "All that the LORD has spoken we will do." And Moses reported the words of the people to the LORD. And the LORD said to Moses, "Behold, I am coming to you in a thick cloud, that the people may hear when I speak with you, and may also believe you forever."

When Moses told the words of the people to the LORD, the LORD said to Moses, "Go to the people and consecrate them today and tomorrow, and let them wash their garments and be ready for the third day. For on the third day the LORD will come down on Mount Sinai in the sight of all the people. And you shall set limits for the people all around, saying, 'Take care not to go up into the mountain or touch the edge of it. Whoever touches the mountain shall be put to death. No hand shall touch him, but he shall be stoned or shot; whether beast or man, he shall not live.' When the trumpet sounds a long blast, they shall come up to the mountain." So Moses went down from the mountain to the people and consecrated the people; and they washed their garments. And he said to the people, "Be ready for the third day; do not go near a woman."

On the morning of the third day there were thunders and lightnings and a thick cloud on the mountain and a very loud trumpet blast, so that all the people in the camp trembled. Then Moses brought the people out of the camp to meet God, and they took their stand at the foot of the mountain. Now Mount Sinai was wrapped in smoke because the LORD had descended on it in fire. The smoke of it went up like the smoke of a kiln, and the whole mountain trembled greatly. And as the sound of the trumpet grew louder and louder, Moses spoke, and God answered him in thunder. The LORD came down on Mount Sinai, to the top of the mountain. And the LORD called Moses to the top of the mountain, and Moses went up.

And the LORD said to Moses, "Go down and warn the people, lest they break through to the LORD to look and many of them perish. Also let the priests who come near to the LORD consecrate themselves, lest the LORD break out against them." And Moses said to the LORD, "The people cannot come up to Mount Sinai, for you yourself warned us, saying, 'Set limits around the mountain and consecrate it.'" And the LORD said to him, "Go down, and come up bringing Aaron with you. But do not let the priests and the people break through to come up to the LORD, lest he break out against them." So Moses went down to the people and told them.

And God spoke all these words, saying,

"I am the LORD your God, who brought you out of the land of Egypt, out of the house of slavery.

"You shall have no other gods before me.

"You shall not make for yourself a carved image, or any likeness of anything that is in heaven above, or that is in the earth beneath, or that is in the water under the earth. You shall not bow down to them or serve them, for I the LORD your God am a jealous God, visiting the iniquity of the fathers on the children to the third and the fourth generation of those who hate me, but showing steadfast love to thousands of those who love me and keep my commandments.

"You shall not take the name of the LORD your God in vain, for the LORD will not hold him guiltless who takes his name in vain.

"Remember the Sabbath day, to keep it holy. Six days you shall labor, and do all your work, but the seventh day is a Sabbath to the LORD your God. On it you shall not do any work, you, or your son, or your daughter, your male servant, or your female servant, or your livestock, or the sojourner who is within your gates. For in six days the LORD made heaven and earth, the sea, and all that is in them, and rested on the seventh day. Therefore the LORD blessed the Sabbath day and made it holy.

"Honor your father and your mother, that your days may be long in the land that the LORD your God is giving you.

"You shall not murder.

"You shall not commit adultery.

"You shall not steal.

"You shall not bear false witness against your neighbor.

"You shall not covet your neighbor's house; you shall not covet your neighbor's wife, or his male servant, or his female servant, or his ox, or his donkey, or anything that is your neighbor's."

The Idolatry of Israel
and the Heart of God

God freed Israel in three movements. He delivered the people from slavery, brought them into a relationship with himself, and gave them instructions to build a tabernacle (a tent) for his presence to be with them. This shows us that God delivers his people in order to dwell with them.

But Israel kept rejecting God. This created a problem: How could this good and holy God dwell with such a rebellious people? God told Moses the answer by revealing his "glory," the beauty of what he is really like. God announced that he is a "God merciful and gracious, slow to anger, and abounding in steadfast love and faithfulness." God also will not "clear the guilty," which means he is right to punish sinners. One day Jesus would come to be punished in the place of sinners so that they could receive this mercy.

M oses said to the LORD, "See, you say to me, 'Bring up this people,' but you have not let me know whom you will send with me. Yet you have said, 'I know you by name, and you have also found favor in my sight.' Now therefore, if I have found favor in your sight, please show me now your ways, that I may know you in order to find favor in your sight. Consider too that this nation is your people." And he said, "My presence will go with you, and I will give you rest." And he said to him, "If your presence will not go with me, do not bring us up from here. For how shall it be known that I have found favor in your sight, I and your people? Is it not in your going with us, so that we are distinct, I and your people, from every other people on the face of the earth?"

And the LORD said to Moses, "This very thing that you have spoken I will do, for you have found favor in my sight, and I know you by name." Moses said, "Please show me your glory." And he said, "I will make all my goodness pass before you and will proclaim before you my name 'The LORD.' And I will be gracious to whom I will be gracious, and will show mercy on whom I will show mercy. But," he said, "you cannot see my face, for man shall not see me and live." And the LORD said, "Behold, there is a place by me where you shall stand on the rock, and while my glory passes by I will put you in a cleft of the rock, and I will cover you with my hand until I have passed by. Then I will take away my hand, and you shall see my back, but my face shall not be seen."

The LORD said to Moses, "Cut for yourself two tablets of stone like the first, and I will write on the tablets the words that were on the first tablets, which you broke. Be ready by the morning, and come up in the morning to Mount Sinai, and present yourself there to me on the top of the mountain. No one shall come up with you, and let no one be seen throughout all the mountain. Let no flocks or herds graze opposite that mountain." So Moses cut two tablets of stone like the first. And he rose early in the morning and went up on Mount Sinai, as the LORD had commanded him, and took in his hand two tablets of stone. The LORD descended in the cloud and stood with him there, and proclaimed the name of the LORD. The LORD passed before him and proclaimed, "The LORD, the LORD, a God merciful and gracious, slow to anger, and abounding in steadfast love and faithfulness, keeping steadfast love for thousands, forgiving iniquity and transgression and sin, but who will by no means clear the guilty, visiting the iniquity of the fathers on the children and the children's children, to the third and the fourth generation." And Moses quickly bowed his head toward the earth and worshiped. And he said, "If now I have found favor in your sight, O Lord, please let the Lord go in the midst of us, for it is a stiff-necked people, and pardon our iniquity and our sin, and take us for your inheritance."

And he said, "Behold, I am making a covenant. Before all your people I will do marvels, such as have not been created in all the earth or in any nation. And all the people among whom you are shall see the work of the LORD, for it is an awesome thing that I will do with you."

Israel's Journey and Rebellion

Moses built the tabernacle, and then God graciously filled it with his presence. He also gave instructions for animal sacrifice, which was the way in which sinners could receive forgiveness and remain right with God. A priest would put his hands on the animal to symbolize the transfer of the person's sins to the animal, and then the animal would die so that the one who gave the sacrifice could live. This pointed forward to the true and greater sacrifice to come, the sacrifice of Jesus.

The tabernacle is about God's presence with his people. It reminds us of the past and points to the future. First, it reminds us of the beginning of the Bible's story, when God dwelt with people in Eden. Second, the tabernacle points forward to the end of the Bible's story, when God will once again dwell with his people—this time forever.

With the tabernacle and sacrifices, Israel set out toward its new home in Canaan. But in the following story from Numbers we see that the people's hearts still had not changed.

At the end of forty days they returned from spying out the land. And they came to Moses and Aaron and to all the congregation of the people of Israel in the wilderness of Paran, at Kadesh. They brought back word to them and to all the congregation, and showed them the fruit of the land. And they told him, "We came to the land to which you sent us. It flows with milk and honey, and this is its fruit. However, the people who dwell in the land are strong, and the cities are fortified and very large. And besides, we saw the descendants of Anak there. The Amalekites dwell in the land of the Negeb. The Hittites, the Jebusites, and the Amorites dwell in the hill country. And the Canaanites dwell by the sea, and along the Jordan."

But Caleb quieted the people before Moses and said, "Let us go up at once and occupy it, for we are well able to overcome it." Then the men who had gone up with him said, "We are not able to go up against the people, for they are stronger than we are." So they brought to the people of Israel a bad report of the land that they had spied out, saying, "The land, through which we have gone to spy it out, is a land that devours its inhabitants, and all the people that we saw in it are of great height. And there we saw the Nephilim (the sons of Anak, who come from the Nephilim), and we seemed to ourselves like grasshoppers, and so we seemed to them."

Then all the congregation raised a loud cry, and the people wept that night. And all the people of Israel grumbled against Moses and Aaron. The whole congregation said to them, "Would that we had died in the land of Egypt! Or would that we had died in this wilderness! Why is the LORD bringing us into this land, to fall by the sword? Our wives and our little ones will become a prey. Would it not be better for us to go back to Egypt?" And they said to one another, "Let us choose a leader and go back to Egypt."

Then Moses and Aaron fell on their faces before all the assembly of the congregation of the people of Israel. And Joshua the son of Nun and Caleb the son of Jephunneh, who were among those who had spied out the land, tore their clothes and said to all the congregation of the people of Israel, "The land, which we passed through to spy it out, is an exceedingly good land. If the LORD delights in us, he will bring us into this land and give it to us, a land that flows with milk and honey. Only do not rebel against the LORD. And do not fear the people of the land, for they are bread for us. Their protection is removed from them, and the LORD is with us; do not fear them." Then all the congregation said to stone them with stones. But the glory of the LORD appeared at the tent of meeting to all the people of Israel.

And the LORD said to Moses, "How long will this people despise me? And how long will they not believe in me, in spite of all the signs that I have done among them? I will strike them with the pestilence and disinherit them, and I will make of you a nation greater and mightier than they."

But Moses said to the LORD, "Then the Egyptians will hear of it, for you brought up this people in your might from among them, and they will tell the inhabitants of this land. They have heard that you, O LORD, are in the midst of this people. For you, O LORD, are seen face to face, and your cloud stands over them and you go before them, in a pillar of cloud by day and in a pillar of fire by night. Now if you kill this people as one man, then the nations who have heard your fame will say, 'It is because the LORD was not able to bring this people into the land that he swore to give to them that he has killed them in the wilderness.' And now, please let the power of the Lord be great as you have promised, saying, 'The LORD is slow to anger and abounding in steadfast love, forgiving iniquity and transgression, but he will by no means clear the guilty, visiting the iniquity of the fathers on the children, to the third and the fourth generation.' Please pardon the iniquity of this people, according to the greatness of your steadfast love, just as you have forgiven this people, from Egypt until now."

Then the LORD said, "I have pardoned, according to your word. But truly, as I live, and as all the earth shall be filled with the glory of the LORD, none of the men who have seen my glory and my signs that I did in Egypt and in the wilderness, and yet have put me to the test these ten times and have not obeyed my voice, shall see the land that I swore to give to their fathers. And none of those who despised me shall see it. But my servant Caleb, because he has a different spirit and has followed me fully, I will bring into the land into which he went, and his descendants shall possess it. Now, since the Amalekites and the Canaanites dwell in the valleys, turn tomorrow and set out for the wilderness by the way to the Red Sea."

Israel Enters the Land

Israel grumbled against God on every step of its journey. Yet God was still patient and kind. When the people grumbled from thirst, he gave them water. When they demanded food, he gave them manna. When they complained about the manna, he sent them quail. Then they rejected God's commands and refused to enter the land of Canaan. They disobeyed God because they did not trust or love him. Therefore God made that first generation wander for forty years.

The book of Joshua tells how the next generation entered and conquered the land of Canaan.

JOSHUA 1:1-11

After the death of Moses the servant of the LORD, the LORD said to Joshua the son of Nun, Moses' assistant, "Moses my servant is dead. Now therefore arise, go over this Jordan, you and all this people, into the land that I am giving to them, to the people of Israel. Every place that the sole of your foot will tread upon I have given to you, just as I promised to Moses. From the wilderness and this Lebanon as far as the great river, the river Euphrates, all the land of the Hittites to the Great Sea toward the going down of the sun shall be your territory. No man shall be able to stand before you all the days of your life. Just as I was with Moses, so I will be with you. I will not leave you or forsake you. Be strong and courageous, for you shall cause this people to inherit the land that I swore to their fathers to give them. Only be strong and very courageous, being careful to do according to all the law that Moses my servant commanded you. Do not turn from it to the right hand or to the left, that you may have good success wherever you go. This Book of the Law shall not depart from your mouth, but you shall meditate on it day and night, so that you may be careful to do according to all that is written in it. For then you will make your way prosperous, and then you will have good success. Have I not commanded you? Be strong and courageous. Do not be frightened, and do not be dismayed, for the LORD your God is with you wherever you go."

And Joshua commanded the officers of the people, "Pass through the midst of the camp and command the people, 'Prepare your provisions, for within three days you are to pass over this Jordan to go in to take possession of the land that the LORD your God is giving you to possess.'"

JOSHUA 3:1–17

Then Joshua rose early in the morning and they set out from Shittim. And they came to the Jordan, he and all the people of Israel, and lodged there before they passed over. At the end of three days the officers went through the camp and commanded the people, "As soon as you see the ark of the covenant of the LORD your God being carried by the Levitical priests, then you shall set out from your place and follow it. Yet there shall be a distance between you and it, about 2,000 cubits in length. Do not come near it, in order that you may know the way you shall go, for you have not passed this way before." Then Joshua said to the people, "Consecrate yourselves, for tomorrow the LORD will do wonders among you." And Joshua said to the priests, "Take up the ark of the covenant and pass on before the people." So they took up the ark of the covenant and went before the people.

The LORD said to Joshua, "Today I will begin to exalt you in the sight of all Israel, that they may know that, as I was with Moses, so I will be with you. And as for you, command the priests who bear the ark of the covenant, 'When you come to the brink of the waters of the Jordan, you shall stand still in the Jordan.'" And Joshua said to the people of Israel, "Come here and listen to the words of the LORD your God." And Joshua said, "Here is how you shall know that the living God is among you and that he will without fail drive out from before you the Canaanites, the Hittites, the Hivites, the Perizzites, the Girgashites, the Amorites, and the Jebusites. Behold, the ark of the covenant of the Lord of all the earth is passing over before you into the Jordan. Now therefore take twelve men from the tribes of Israel, from each tribe a man. And when the soles of the feet of the priests bearing the ark of the LORD, the Lord of all the earth, shall rest in the waters of the Jordan, the waters of the Jordan shall be cut off from flowing, and the waters coming down from above shall stand in one heap."

So when the people set out from their tents to pass over the Jordan with the priests bearing the ark of the covenant before the people, and as soon as those bearing the ark had come as far as the Jordan, and the feet of the priests bearing the ark were dipped in the brink of the water (now the Jordan overflows all its banks throughout the time of harvest), the waters coming down from above stood and rose up in a heap very far away, at Adam, the city that is beside Zarethan, and those flowing down toward the Sea of the Arabah, the Salt Sea, were completely cut off. And the people passed over opposite Jericho. Now the priests bearing the ark of the covenant of the LORD stood firmly on dry ground in the midst of the Jordan, and all Israel was passing over on dry ground until all the nation finished passing over the Jordan.

Part 3

GOD'S KINGDOM
ESTABLISHED

Israel's Cycle of Sin
and Restoration

As part of God's plan to rescue sinners and restore creation, he promised to make Abraham's descendants a great nation and to give them the land of Canaan. The book of Joshua shows how God blessed Israel with his protection and presence in the land. This reminds us of Eden, when man and woman were at rest in the garden, experiencing peace in God's presence. Canaan is even described as a wonderful place like Eden.

Yet, like Adam and Eve, Israel did not trust or obey God. Judges shows that Israel "did what was evil in the sight of the Lord." This next reading is an example of how Israel's situation kept getting worse. Yet God continued to be merciful and patient with his people.

JUDGES 2:1–23

Now the angle of the Lord went up from Gilgal to Bochim. And he said, "I brought you up from Egypt and brought you into the land that I swore to give to your fathers. I said, 'I will never break my covenant with you, and you shall make no covenant with the inhabitants of this land; you shall break down their altars.' But you have not obeyed my voice. What is this you have done? So now I say, I will not drive them out before you, but they shall become thorns in your sides, and their gods shall be a snare to you." As soon as the angel of the Lord spoke these words to all the people of Israel, the people lifted up their voices and wept. And they called the name of that place Bochim. And they sacrificed there to the Lord.

When Joshua dismissed the people, the people of Israel went each to his inheritance to take possession of the land. And the people served the Lord all the days of Joshua, and all the days of the elders who outlived Joshua, who had seen all the great work that the Lord had done for Israel. And Joshua the son of Nun, the servant of the Lord, died at the age of 110 years. And they buried him within the boundaries of his inheritance in Timnath-heres, in the hill country of Ephraim, north of the mountain of Gaash. And all that generation also were gathered to their fathers. And there arose another generation after them who did not know the LORD or the work that he had done for Israel.

And the people of Israel did what was evil in the sight of the LORD and served the Baals. And they abandoned the LORD, the God of their fathers, who had brought them out of the land of Egypt. They went after other gods, from among the gods of the peoples who were around them, and bowed down to them. And they provoked the LORD to anger. They abandoned the LORD and served the Baals and the Ashtaroth. So the anger of the LORD was kindled against Israel, and he gave them over to plunderers, who plundered them. And he sold them into the hand of their surrounding enemies, so that they could no longer withstand their enemies. Whenever they marched out, the hand of the LORD was against them for harm, as the LORD had warned, and as the LORD had sworn to them. And they were in terrible distress.

Then the LORD raised up judges, who saved them out of the hand of those who plundered them. Yet they did not listen to their judges, for they whored after other gods and bowed down to them. They soon turned aside from the way in which their fathers had walked, who had obeyed the commandments of the LORD, and they did not do so. Whenever the LORD raised up judges for them, the LORD was with the judge, and he saved them from the hand of their enemies all the days of the judge. For the LORD was moved to pity by their groaning because of those who afflicted and oppressed them. But whenever the judge died, they turned back and were more corrupt than their fathers, going after other gods, serving them and bowing down to them. They did not drop any of their practices or their stubborn ways. So the anger of the LORD was kindled against Israel, and he said, "Because this people have transgressed my covenant that I commanded their fathers and have not obeyed my voice, I will no longer drive out before them any of the nations that Joshua left when he died, in order to test Israel by them, whether they will take care to walk in the way of the LORD as their fathers did, or not." So the LORD left those nations, not driving them out quickly, and he did not give them into the hand of Joshua.

Israel Needs a King

Israel repeated a disappointing pattern many times. (1) The people committed idolatry by trusting and worshiping false gods. (2) God punished them by handing them over to their enemies. (3) God graciously raised up a judge to rescue them. (4) Israel once again abandoned the Lord when the judge died. As we read about how sinful Israel was, we also see how sinful all people are. And this makes us ask questions: Is there any hope? Will Israel remain in the land? Or will God send the nation out, as he did Adam and Eve?

Accounts like this next one at the end of Judges include a few statements that tell us what Israel needed: "In those days there was no king in Israel. Everyone did what was right in his own eyes." Israel needed a king.

Now the men of Israel had sworn at Mizpah, "No one of us shall give his daughter in marriage to Benjamin." And the people came to Bethel and sat there till evening before God, and they lifted up their voices and wept bitterly. And they said, "O LORD, the God of Israel, why has this happened in Israel, that today there should be one tribe lacking in Israel?" And the next day the people rose early and built there an altar and offered burnt offerings and peace offerings. And the people of Israel said, "Which of all the tribes of Israel did not come up in the assembly to the LORD?" For they had taken a great oath concerning him who did not come up to the LORD to Mizpah, saying, "He shall surely be put to death." And the people of Israel had compassion for Benjamin their brother and said, "One tribe is cut off from Israel this day. What shall we do for wives for those who are left, since we have sworn by the LORD that we will not give them any of our daughters for wives?"

And they said, "What one is there of the tribes of Israel that did not come up to the LORD to Mizpah?" And behold, no one had come to the camp from Jabesh-gilead, to the assembly. For when the people were mustered, behold, not one of the inhabitants of Jabesh-gilead was there. So the congregation sent 12,000 of their bravest men there and commanded them, "Go and strike the inhabitants of Jabesh-gilead with the edge of the sword; also the women and the little ones. This is what you shall do: every male and every woman that has lain with a male you shall devote to destruction." And they found among the inhabitants of Jabesh-gilead 400 young virgins who had not known a man by lying with him, and they brought them to the camp at Shiloh, which is in the land of Canaan.

Then the whole congregation sent word to the people of Benjamin who were at the rock of Rimmon and proclaimed peace to them. And Benjamin returned at that time. And they gave them the women whom they had saved alive of the women of Jabesh-gilead, but they were not enough for them. And the people had compassion on Benjamin because the LORD had made a breach in the tribes of Israel.

Then the elders of the congregation said, "What shall we do for wives for those who are left, since the women are destroyed out of Benjamin?" And they said, "There must be an inheritance for the survivors of Benjamin, that a tribe not be blotted out from Israel. Yet we cannot give them wives from our daughters." For the people of Israel had sworn, "Cursed be he who gives a wife to Benjamin." So they said, "Behold, there is the yearly feast of the LORD at Shiloh, which is north of Bethel, on the east of the highway that goes up from Bethel to Shechem, and south of Lebonah." And they commanded the people of Benjamin, saying, "Go and lie in ambush in the vineyards and watch. If the daughters of Shiloh come out to dance in the dances, then come out of the vineyards and snatch each man his wife from the daughters of Shiloh, and go to the land of Benjamin. And when their fathers or their brothers come to complain to us, we will say to them, 'Grant them graciously to us, because we did not take for each man of them his wife in battle, neither did you give them to them, else you would now be guilty.'" And the people of Benjamin did so and took their wives, according to their number, from the dancers whom they carried off. Then they went and returned to their inheritance and rebuilt the towns and lived in them. And the people of Israel departed from there at that time, every man to his tribe and family, and they went out from there every man to his inheritance.

In those days there was no king in Israel. Everyone did what was right in his own eyes.

Israel Receives a King

Israel needed a king. This was not entirely unexpected. Genesis had promised that God would send a king through Abraham's line to defeat evil and restore blessing to the world.

But when Israel asked for a king, God did not approve! Why not? Because the Israelites did not want a king who would help them trust God. They wanted a king *instead* of God! Yet the Lord graciously provided a king anyway. He did so because it was all part of his plan to bless his people in the end.

The next readings show God's gift of kingship to Israel and the appointment of Saul as its first king. This continues God's plan eventually to send a true and better King—Jesus. The Bible continues to show us God's never-ending commitment to bless his people.

S amuel judged Israel all the days of his life. And he went on a circuit year by year to Bethel, Gilgal, and Mizpah. And he judged Israel in all these places. Then he would return to Ramah, for his home was there, and there also he judged Israel. And he built there an altar to the LORD.

When Samuel became old, he made his sons judges over Israel. The name of his firstborn son was Joel, and the name of his second, Abijah; they were judges in Beersheba. Yet his sons did not walk in his ways but turned aside after gain. They took bribes and perverted justice.

Then all the elders of Israel gathered together and came to Samuel at Ramah and said to him, "Behold, you are old and your sons do not walk in your ways. Now appoint for us a king to judge us like all the nations." But the thing displeased Samuel when they said, "Give us a king to judge us." And Samuel prayed to the LORD. And the LORD said to Samuel, "Obey the voice of the people in all that they say to you, for they have not rejected you, but they have rejected me from being king over them. According to all the deeds that they have done, from the day I brought them up out of Egypt even to this day, forsaking me and serving other gods, so they are also doing to you. Now then, obey their voice; only you shall solemnly warn them and show them the ways of the king who shall reign over them."

So Samuel told all the words of the LORD to the people who were asking for a king from him. He said, "These will be the ways of the king who will reign over you: he will take your sons and appoint them to his chariots and to be his horsemen and to run before his chariots. And he will appoint for himself commanders of thousands and commanders of fifties, and some to plow his ground and to reap his harvest, and to make his implements of war and the equipment of his chariots. He will take your daughters to be perfumers and cooks and bakers. He will take the best of your fields and vineyards and olive orchards and give them to his servants. He will take the tenth of your grain and of your vineyards and give it to his officers and to his servants. He will take your male servants and female servants and the best of your young men and your donkeys, and put them to his work. He will take the tenth of your flocks, and you shall be his slaves. And in that day you will cry out because of your king, whom you have chosen for yourselves, but the LORD will not answer you in that day."

But the people refused to obey the voice of Samuel. And they said, "No! But there shall be a king over us, that we also may be like all the nations, and that our king may judge us and go out before us and fight our battles." And when Samuel had heard all the words of the people, he repeated them in the ears of the LORD. And the LORD said to Samuel, "Obey their voice and make them a king." Samuel then said to the men of Israel, "Go every man to his city."

Now Samuel called the people together to the LORD at Mizpah. And he said to the people of Israel, "Thus says the LORD, the God of Israel, 'I brought up Israel out of Egypt, and I delivered you from the hand of the Egyptians and from the hand of all the kingdoms that were oppressing you.' But today you have rejected your God, who saves you from all your calamities and your distresses, and you have said to him, 'Set a king over us.' Now therefore present yourselves before the LORD by your tribes and by your thousands."

Then Samuel brought all the tribes of Israel near, and the tribe of Benjamin was taken by lot. He brought the tribe of Benjamin near by its clans, and the clan of the Matrites was taken by lot; and Saul the son of Kish was taken by lot. But when they sought him, he could not be found. So they inquired again of the LORD, "Is there a man still to come?" and the LORD said, "Behold, he has hidden himself among the baggage." Then they ran and took him from there. And when he stood among the people, he was taller than any of the people from his shoulders upward. And Samuel said to all the people, "Do you see him whom the LORD has chosen? There is none like him among all the people." And all the people shouted, "Long live the king!"

Then Samuel told the people the rights and duties of the kingship, and he wrote them in a book and laid it up before the LORD. Then Samuel sent all the people away, each one to his home. Saul also went to his home at Gibeah, and with him went men of valor whose hearts God had touched. But some worthless fellows said,

"How can this man save us?" And they despised him and brought him no present. But he held his peace.

The Rejection of Saul
and Anointing of David

Israel's first king was Saul. He was tall, handsome, and wealthy. But he did not have what matters most to God: humility. He did not trust God, nor was he committed to obeying God. Because Saul failed, the prophet Samuel showed that David would be Israel's next king.

This next account shows us the difference between what the world values and what God values. This battle between David and Goliath does not teach us how we can face giants like David did. Instead, this text shows us how God rescues his helpless people through his humble, faith-filled king. In the beginning of the Bible's story we read of a conflict between the offspring of Eve and the offspring of Satan. Here we see this conflict played out, as God's chosen king conquers the Serpent-like giant.

David pictures how God would ultimately rescue his people through Jesus. The cross where Jesus died looks like weakness, but it was how God accomplished his victory. It looked like Jesus was weak, but he defeated sin, death, and Satan for us. As we see David defeat Goliath, we are reminded of how Jesus has rescued us.

1 SAMUEL 17:1–54

Now the Philistines gathered their armies for battle. And they were gathered at Socoh, which belongs to Judah, and encamped between Socoh and Azekah, in Ephes-dammim. And Saul and the men of Israel were gathered, and encamped in the Valley of Elah, and drew up in line of battle against the Philistines. And the Philistines stood on the mountain on the one side, and Israel stood on the mountain on the other side, with a valley between them. And there came out from the camp of the Philistines a champion named Goliath of Gath, whose height was six cubits and a span. He had a helmet of bronze on his head, and he was armed with a coat of mail, and the weight of the coat was five thousand shekels of bronze. And he had bronze armor on his legs, and a javelin of bronze slung between his shoulders. The shaft of his spear was like a weaver's beam, and his spear's head weighed six hundred shekels of iron. And his shield-bearer went before him. He stood and shouted to the ranks of Israel, "Why have you come out to draw up for battle? Am I not a Philistine, and are you not servants of Saul? Choose a man for yourselves, and let him come down to me. If he is able to fight with me and kill me, then we will be your servants. But if I prevail against him and kill him, then you shall be our servants and serve us." And the

Philistine said, "I defy the ranks of Israel this day. Give me a man, that we may fight together." When Saul and all Israel heard these words of the Philistine, they were dismayed and greatly afraid.

Now David was the son of an Ephrathite of Bethlehem in Judah, named Jesse, who had eight sons. In the days of Saul the man was already old and advanced in years. The three oldest sons of Jesse had followed Saul to the battle. And the names of his three sons who went to the battle were Eliab the firstborn, and next to him Abinadab, and the third Shammah. David was the youngest. The three eldest followed Saul, but David went back and forth from Saul to feed his father's sheep at Bethlehem. For forty days the Philistine came forward and took his stand, morning and evening.

And Jesse said to David his son, "Take for your brothers an ephah of this parched grain, and these ten loaves, and carry them quickly to the camp to your brothers. Also take these ten cheeses to the commander of their thousand. See if your brothers are well, and bring some token from them."

Now Saul and they and all the men of Israel were in the Valley of Elah, fighting with the Philistines. And David rose early in the morning and left the sheep with a keeper and took the provisions and went, as Jesse had commanded him. And he came to the encampment as the host was going out to the battle line, shouting the war cry. And Israel and the Philistines drew up for battle, army against army. And David left the things in charge of the keeper of the baggage and ran to the ranks and went and greeted his brothers. As he talked with them, behold, the champion, the

Philistine of Gath, Goliath by name, came up out of the ranks of the Philistines and spoke the same words as before. And David heard him.

All the men of Israel, when they saw the man, fled from him and were much afraid. And the men of Israel said, "Have you seen this man who has come up? Surely he has come up to defy Israel. And the king will enrich the man who kills him with great riches and will give him his daughter and make his father's house free in Israel." And David said to the men who stood by him, "What shall be done for the man who kills this Philistine and takes away the reproach from Israel? For who is this uncircumcised Philistine, that he should defy the armies of the living God?" And the people answered him in the same way, "So shall it be done to the man who kills him."

Now Eliab his eldest brother heard when he spoke to the men. And Eliab's anger was kindled against David, and he said, "Why have you come down? And with whom have you left those few sheep in the wilderness? I know your presumption and the evil of your heart, for you have come down to see the battle." And David said, "What have I done now? Was it not but a word?" And he turned away from him toward another, and spoke in the same way, and the people answered him again as before.

When the words that David spoke were heard, they repeated them before Saul, and he sent for him. And David said to Saul, "Let no man's heart fail because of him. Your servant will go and fight with this Philistine." And Saul said to David, "You are not able to go against this Philistine to fight with him, for you are but a youth, and he has been a man of war from his youth." But David said to Saul, "Your servant used to keep sheep for his father. And when there came a lion, or a bear, and took a lamb from the flock, I went after him and struck him and delivered it out of his mouth. And if he arose against me, I caught him by his beard and struck him and killed him. Your servant has struck down both lions and bears, and this uncircumcised Philistine shall be like one of them, for he has defied the armies of the living God." And David said, "The LORD who delivered me from the paw of the lion and from the paw of the bear will deliver me from the hand of this Philistine." And Saul said to David, "Go, and the LORD be with you!"

Then Saul clothed David with his armor. He put a helmet of bronze on his head and clothed him with a coat of mail, and David strapped his sword over his armor. And he tried in vain to go, for he had not tested them. Then David said to Saul, "I cannot go with these, for I have not tested them." So David put them off. Then he took his staff in his hand and chose five smooth stones from the brook and put them in his shepherd's pouch. His sling was in his hand, and he approached the Philistine.

And the Philistine moved forward and came near to David, with his shield-bearer in front of him. And when the Philistine looked and saw David, he disdained him, for he was but a youth, ruddy and handsome in appearance. And the Philistine said to David, "Am I a dog, that you come to me with sticks?" And the Philistine cursed David by his gods. The Philistine said to David, "Come to me, and I will give your flesh to the birds of the air and to the beasts of the field." Then David said to the Philistine, "You come to me with a sword and with a spear and with a javelin, but I come to you in the name of the LORD of hosts, the God of the armies of Israel, whom you have defied. This day the LORD will deliver you into my hand, and I will strike you down and cut off your head. And I will give the dead bodies of the host of the Philistines this day to the birds of the air and to the wild beasts of the earth, that all the earth may know that there is a God in Israel, and that all this assembly may know that the LORD saves not with sword and spear. For the battle is the LORD's, and he will give you into our hand."

When the Philistine arose and came and drew near to meet David, David ran quickly toward the battle line to meet the Philistine. And David put his hand in his bag and took out a stone and slung it and struck the Philistine on his forehead. The stone sank into his forehead, and he fell on his face to the ground.

So David prevailed over the Philistine with a sling and with a stone, and struck the Philistine and killed him. There was no sword in the hand of David. Then David ran and stood over the Philistine and took his sword and drew it out of its sheath and killed him and cut off his head with it. When the Philistines saw that their champion was dead, they fled. And the men of Israel and Judah rose with a shout and pursued the Philistines as far as Gath and the gates of Ekron, so that the wounded Philistines fell on the way from Shaaraim as far as Gath and Ekron. And the people of Israel came back from chasing the Philistines, and they plundered their camp. And David took the head of the Philistine and brought it to Jerusalem, but he put his armor in his tent.

The Covenant with David

Rather than acknowledging David as the next king, Saul became jealous and tried to kill him. Although David had to live for many years on the run in the wilderness, the Lord repeatedly delivered him from Saul. David then became king after Saul died. The pattern of David's life would later become the pattern of Jesus' (and the pattern for all who follow Jesus): suffering first, then glory.

In the next reading God promises that David's kingdom will never end. We call this the Davidic covenant. Over time we learn that God will not just keep giving Israel kings from David's line; he will give them one true King who will rule forever. This King will come to remove the sin and suffering of the world. He will be the one to bring to the world the blessing that God promised Abraham. He will make the world like Eden again, but better.

2 SAMUEL 7:1–29

Now when the king lived in his house and the LORD had given him rest from all his surrounding enemies, the king said to Nathan the prophet, "See now, I dwell in a house of cedar, but the ark of God dwells in a tent." And Nathan said to the king, "Go, do all that is in your heart, for the LORD is with you."

But that same night the word of the LORD came to Nathan, "Go and tell my servant David, 'Thus says the LORD: Would you build me a house to dwell in? I have not lived in a house since the day I brought up the people of Israel from Egypt to this day, but I have been moving about in a tent for my dwelling. In all places where I have moved with all the people of Israel, did I speak a word with any of the judges of Israel, whom I commanded to shepherd my people Israel, saying, "Why have you not built me a house of cedar?" ' Now, therefore, thus you shall say to my servant David, 'Thus says the LORD of hosts, I took you from the pasture, from following the sheep, that you should be prince over my people Israel. And I have been with you wherever you went and have cut off all your enemies from before you. And I will make for you a great name, like the name of the great ones of the earth. And I will appoint a place for my people Israel and will plant them, so that they may dwell in their own place and be disturbed no more.

And violent men shall afflict them no more, as formerly, from the time that I appointed judges over my people Israel. And I will give you rest from all your enemies. Moreover, the LORD declares to you that the LORD will make you a house. When your days are fulfilled and you lie down with your fathers, I will raise up your offspring after you, who shall come from your body, and I will establish his kingdom. He shall build a house for my name, and I will establish the throne of his kingdom forever. I will be to him a father, and he shall be to me a son. When he commits iniquity, I will discipline him with the rod of men, with the stripes of the sons of men, but my steadfast love will not depart from him, as I took it from Saul, whom I put away from before you. And your house and your kingdom shall be made sure forever before me. Your throne shall be established forever.'" In accordance with all these words, and in accordance with all this vision, Nathan spoke to David.

Then King David went in and sat before the LORD and said, "Who am I, O Lord GOD, and what is my house, that you have brought me thus far? And yet this was a small thing in your eyes, O Lord GOD. You have spoken also of your servant's house for a great while to come, and this is instruction for mankind, O Lord GOD! And what more can David say to you? For you know your servant, O Lord GOD! Because of your promise, and according to your own heart, you have brought about all this greatness, to make your servant know it. Therefore you are great, O LORD God. For there is none like you, and there is no God besides you, according to all that we have heard with our ears. And who is like your people Israel, the one nation on earth whom God went to redeem to be his people, making himself a name and doing for them great and awesome things by driving out before your people, whom you redeemed for yourself from Egypt, a nation and its gods? And you established for yourself your people Israel to be your people forever. And you, O LORD, became their God. And now, O LORD God, confirm forever the word that you have spoken concerning your servant and concerning his house, and do as you have spoken. And your name will be magnified forever, saying, 'The LORD of hosts is God over Israel,' and the house of your servant David will be established before you. For you, O LORD of hosts, the God of Israel, have made this revelation to your servant, saying, 'I will build you a house.' Therefore your servant has found courage to pray this prayer to you. And now, O Lord GOD, you are God, and your words are true, and you have promised this good thing to your servant. Now therefore may it please you to bless the house of your servant, so that it may continue forever before you. For you, O Lord GOD, have spoken, and with your blessing shall the house of your servant be blessed forever."

The Kingdom Established through Solomon

David was a good king. But he was also like every other person in this way: he had a sinful nature. He knew what it was like to do terrible things and then try to hide his sin. But God loved him and led him to repentance, which means turning from sin. David was a sinner, but he lived with the joy of knowing God's grace and forgiveness.

All of David's failures remind us that we need a better king. In this next section we see David's son Solomon become Israel's next king. Israel experienced great blessing under Solomon's rule. This era reminds us of Eden, where we saw God's people in God's place, enjoying his presence and rule.

King David said, "Call to me Zadok the priest, Nathan the prophet, and Benaiah the son of Jehoiada." So they came before the king. And the king said to them, "Take with you the servants of your lord and have Solomon my son ride on my own mule, and bring him down to Gihon. And let Zadok the priest and Nathan the prophet there anoint him king over Israel. Then blow the trumpet and say, 'Long live King Solomon!' You shall then come up after him, and he shall come and sit on my throne, for he shall be king in my place. And I have appointed him to be ruler over Israel and over Judah." And Benaiah the son of Jehoiada answered the king, "Amen! May the LORD, the God of my lord the king, say so. As the LORD has been with my lord the king, even so may he be with Solomon, and make his throne greater than the throne of my lord King David."

So Zadok the priest, Nathan the prophet, and Benaiah the son of Jehoiada, and the Cherethites and the Pelethites went down and had Solomon ride on King David's mule and brought him to Gihon. There Zadok the priest took the horn of oil from the tent and anointed Solomon. Then they blew the trumpet, and all the people said, "Long live King Solomon!" And all the people went up after him, playing on pipes, and rejoicing with great joy, so that the earth was split by their noise.

1 KINGS 4:20–34

Judah and Israel were as many as the sand by the sea. They ate and drank and were happy. Solomon ruled over all the kingdoms from the Euphrates to the land of the Philistines and to the border of Egypt. They brought tribute and served Solomon all the days of his life.

Solomon's provision for one day was thirty cors of fine flour and sixty cors of meal, ten fat oxen, and twenty pasture-fed cattle, a hundred sheep, besides deer, gazelles, roebucks, and fattened fowl. For he had dominion over all the region west of the Euphrates from Tiphsah to Gaza, over all the kings west of the Euphrates. And he had peace on all sides around him. And Judah and Israel lived in safety, from Dan even to Beersheba, every man under his vine and under his fig tree, all the days of Solomon. Solomon also had 40,000 stalls of horses for his chariots, and 12,000 horsemen. And those officers supplied provisions for King Solomon, and for all who came to King Solomon's table, each one in his month. They let nothing be lacking. Barley also and straw for the horses and swift steeds they brought to the place where it was required, each according to his duty.

And God gave Solomon wisdom and understanding beyond measure, and breadth of mind like the sand on the seashore, so that Solomon's wisdom surpassed the wisdom of all the people of the east and all the wisdom of Egypt. For he was wiser than all other men, wiser than Ethan the Ezrahite, and Heman, Calcol, and Darda, the sons of Mahol, and his fame was in all the surrounding nations. He also spoke 3,000 proverbs, and his songs were 1,005. He spoke of trees, from the cedar that is in Lebanon to the hyssop that grows out of the wall. He spoke also of beasts, and of birds, and of reptiles, and of fish. And people of all nations came to hear the wisdom of Solomon, and from all the kings of the earth, who had heard of his wisdom.

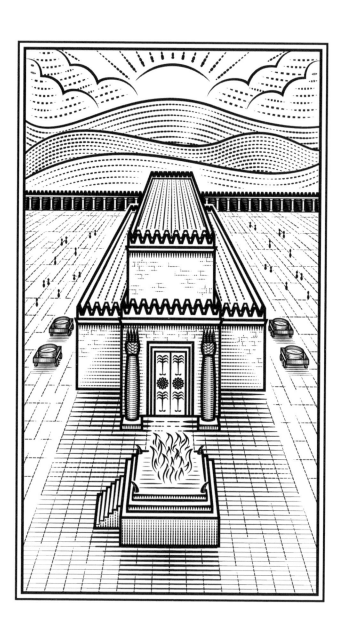

The Temple Built by Solomon

Israel had come a long way since its slavery in Egypt. Under Solomon's rule the kingdom looked more and more like Eden. Like Adam and Eve, the Israelites were God's people in God's land, blessed with God's presence and good commands. Solomon also built a temple in Jerusalem that was in many ways a symbol of Eden. It was the place where people received forgiveness and experienced God's presence.

This temple reminds us of Eden and looks forward to a new creation. It points forward to the coming day when God will dwell with his people in a new paradise forever. We will not need a temple then, because God will be with us.

Then Solomon assembled the elders of Israel and all the heads of the tribes, the leaders of the fathers' houses of the people of Israel, before King Solomon in Jerusalem, to bring up the ark of the covenant of the LORD out of the city of David, which is Zion. And all the men of Israel assembled to King Solomon at the feast in the month Ethanim, which is the seventh month. And all the elders of Israel came, and the priests took up the ark. And they brought up the ark of the LORD, the tent of meeting, and all the holy vessels that were in the tent; the priests and the Levites brought them up. And King Solomon and all the congregation of Israel, who had assembled before him, were with him before the ark, sacrificing so many sheep and oxen that they could not be counted or numbered. Then the priests brought the ark of the covenant of the LORD to its place in the inner sanctuary of the house, in the Most Holy Place, underneath the wings of the cherubim. For the cherubim spread out their wings over the place of the ark, so that the cherubim overshadowed the ark and its poles. And the poles were so long that the ends of the poles were seen from the Holy Place before the inner sanctuary; but they could not be seen from outside. And they are there to this day. There was nothing in the ark except the two tablets of stone that Moses put there at Horeb, where the LORD made a covenant with the people of Israel, when they came out of the land of Egypt. And when the priests came out of the Holy Place, a cloud filled the house of the LORD, so that the priests could not stand to minister because of the cloud, for the glory of the LORD filled the house of the LORD.

Then Solomon said, "The LORD has said that he would dwell in thick darkness. I have indeed built you an exalted house, a place for you to dwell in forever." Then the king turned around and blessed all the assembly of Israel, while all the assembly of Israel stood. And he said, "Blessed be the LORD, the God of Israel, who with his hand has fulfilled what he promised with his mouth to David my father, saying, 'Since the day that I brought my people Israel out of Egypt, I chose no city out of all the tribes of Israel in which to build a house, that my name might be there. But I chose David to be over my people Israel.' Now it was in the heart of David my father to build a house for the name of the LORD, the God of Israel. But the LORD said to David my father, 'Whereas it was in your heart to build a house for my name, you did well that it was in your heart. Nevertheless, you shall not build the house, but your son who shall be born to you shall build the house for my name.' Now the LORD has fulfilled his promise that he made. For I have risen in the place of David my father, and sit on the throne of Israel, as the LORD promised, and I have built the house for the name of the LORD, the God of Israel. And there I have provided a place for the ark, in which is the covenant of the LORD that he made with our fathers, when he brought them out of the land of Egypt."

Then Solomon stood before the altar of the LORD in the presence of all the assembly of Israel and spread out his hands toward heaven, and said, "O LORD, God of Israel, there is no God like you, in heaven above or on earth beneath, keeping covenant and showing steadfast love to your servants who walk before you with all their heart; you have kept with your servant David my father what you declared to him. You spoke with your mouth, and with your hand have fulfilled it this day. Now therefore, O LORD, God of Israel, keep for your servant David my father what you have promised him, saying, 'You shall not lack a man to sit before me on the throne of Israel, if only your sons pay close attention to their way, to walk before me as you have walked before me.' Now therefore, O God of Israel, let your word be confirmed, which you have spoken to your servant David my father.

"But will God indeed dwell on the earth? Behold, heaven and the highest heaven cannot contain you; how much less this house that I have built! Yet have regard to the prayer of your servant and to his plea, O LORD my God, listening to the cry and to the prayer that your servant prays before you this day, that your eyes may be open night and day toward this house, the place of which you have said, 'My name shall be there,' that you may listen to the prayer that your servant offers toward this place. And listen to the plea of your servant and of your people Israel, when they pray toward this place. And listen in heaven your dwelling place, and when you hear, forgive."

Part 4

GOD'S KINGDOM DECLINED AND PARTIALLY RESTORED

The Kingdom Divided

God brought Israel to a high point during Solomon's reign. He gave his people land to dwell in, a king to rule them, and a temple with sacrifices in order to find forgiveness for sins. But this blessing did not continue, due to Israel's unfaithfulness. It was at this very point that the kingdom began to unravel. Although God blessed Israel with a great kingdom, the people's hearts did not love God or love their neighbors well. King Solomon and Israel turned away from the Lord.

The united kingdom of Israel's twelve tribes divided into two kingdoms. God was continually kind to his people, but the problem of their sinful hearts was deep. Israel's history shows that no amount of material blessing could make a sinful heart love God. Our world needed a true king and new hearts. That day would come with Jesus, but Israel first had to enter into a time of judgment for its sin.

1 KINGS 11:1–13

Now King Solomon loved many foreign women, along with the daughter of Pharaoh: Moabite, Ammonite, Edomite, Sidonian, and Hittite women, from the nations concerning which the LORD had said to the people of Israel, "You shall not enter into marriage with them, neither shall they with you, for surely they will turn away your heart after their gods." Solomon clung to these in love. He had 700 wives, who were princesses, and 300 concubines. And his wives turned away his heart. For when Solomon was old his wives turned away his heart after other gods, and his heart was not wholly true to the LORD his God, as was the heart of David his father. For Solomon went after Ashtoreth the goddess of the Sidonians, and after Milcom the abomination of the Ammonites. So Solomon did what was evil in the sight of the LORD and did not wholly follow the LORD, as David his father had done. Then Solomon built a high place for Chemosh the abomination of Moab, and for Molech the abomination of the Ammonites, on the mountain east of Jerusalem. And so he did for all his foreign wives, who made offerings and sacrificed to their gods.

And the LORD was angry with Solomon, because his heart had turned away from the LORD, the God of Israel, who had appeared to him twice and had commanded him concerning this thing, that he should not go after other gods. But he did not keep what the LORD commanded. Therefore the LORD said to Solomon, "Since this has been your practice and you have not kept my covenant and my statutes that I have commanded you, I will surely tear the kingdom from you and will give it to your servant. Yet for the sake of David your father I will not do it in your days, but I will tear it out of the hand of your son. However, I will not tear away all the kingdom, but I will give one tribe to your son, for the sake of David my servant and for the sake of Jerusalem that I have chosen."

1 KINGS 12:1–20

Rehoboam went to Shechem, for all Israel had come to Shechem to make him king. And as soon as Jeroboam the son of Nebat heard of it (for he was still in Egypt, where he had fled from King Solomon), then Jeroboam returned from Egypt. And they sent and called him, and Jeroboam and all the assembly of Israel came and said to Rehoboam, "Your father made our yoke heavy. Now therefore lighten the hard service of your father and his heavy yoke on us, and we will serve you." He said to them, "Go away for three days, then come again to me." So the people went away.

Then King Rehoboam took counsel with the old men, who had stood before Solomon his father while he was yet alive, saying, "How do you advise me to answer this people?" And they said to him, "If you will be a servant to this people today and serve them, and speak good words to them when you answer them, then they will be your servants forever." But he abandoned the counsel that the old men gave him and took counsel with the young men who had grown up with him and stood before him. And he said to them, "What do you advise that we answer this people who have said to me, 'Lighten the yoke that your father put on us'?" And the young men who had grown up with him said to him, "Thus shall you speak to this people who said to you, 'Your father made our yoke heavy, but you lighten it for us,' thus shall you say to them, 'My little finger is thicker than my father's thighs. And now, whereas my father laid on you a heavy yoke, I will add to your yoke. My father disciplined you with whips, but I will discipline you with scorpions.'"

So Jeroboam and all the people came to Rehoboam the third day, as the king said, "Come to me again the third day." And the king answered the people harshly, and forsaking the counsel that the old men had given him, he spoke to them according to the counsel of the young men, saying, "My father made your yoke heavy, but I will add to your yoke. My father disciplined you with whips, but I will discipline you with scorpions." So the king did not listen to the people, for it was a turn of affairs brought about by the LORD that he might fulfill his word, which the LORD spoke by Ahijah the Shilonite to Jeroboam the son of Nebat.

And when all Israel saw that the king did not listen to them, the people answered the king, "What portion do we have in David? We have no inheritance in the son of Jesse. To your tents, O Israel! Look now to your own house, David." So Israel went to their tents.

But Rehoboam reigned over the people of Israel who lived in the cities of Judah. Then King Rehoboam sent Adoram, who was taskmaster over the forced labor, and all Israel stoned him to death with stones. And King Rehoboam hurried to mount his chariot to flee to Jerusalem. So Israel has been in rebellion against the house of David to this day. And when all Israel heard that Jeroboam had returned, they sent and called him to the assembly and made him king over all Israel. There was none that followed the house of David but the tribe of Judah only.

Judah Exiled

The kingdom of Israel quickly divided after Solomon's death. The ten northern tribes split from the two southern tribes. This created two kingdoms: the northern kingdom, called Israel, and the southern kingdom, called Judah.

The northern kingdom of Israel followed unfaithful kings and worshiped idols rather than God. God eventually judged Israel with exile in 722 BC, which means that he sent the people out of their land. The Assyrians defeated and carried away many Israelites. Then the southern kingdom of Judah also rejected God. This next text shows how God used the powerful kingdom of Babylon to send Judah into exile in 586 BC.

Exile means leaving the place of God's presence and blessing. Israel's exile was like Adam's original exile from Eden. It also reminds us that every human being is born into this world exiled and separated from God. But we have hope: the God who rightly sent us out is the God who would one day bring us home through Jesus.

2 KINGS 25:1–21

A nd in the ninth year of his reign, in the tenth month, on the tenth day of the month, Nebuchadnezzar king of Babylon came with all his army against Jerusalem and laid siege to it. And they built siegeworks all around it. So the city was besieged till the eleventh year of King Zedekiah. On the ninth day of the fourth month the famine was so severe in the city that there was no food for the people of the land. Then a breach was made in the city, and all the men of war fled by night by the way of the gate between the two walls, by the king's garden, and the Chaldeans were around the city. And they went in the direction of the Arabah. But the army of the Chaldeans pursued the king and overtook him in the plains of Jericho, and all his army was scattered from him. Then they captured the king and brought him up to the king of Babylon at Riblah, and they passed sentence on him. They slaughtered the sons of Zedekiah before his eyes, and put out the eyes of Zedekiah and bound him in chains and took him to Babylon.

In the fifth month, on the seventh day of the month—that was the nineteenth year of King Nebuchadnezzar, king of Babylon— Nebuzaradan, the captain of the bodyguard, a servant of the king of Babylon, came to Jerusalem. And he burned the house of the LORD and the king's house and all the houses of Jerusalem; every great house he burned down. And all the army of the Chaldeans, who were with the captain of the guard, broke down the walls around Jerusalem. And the rest of the people who were left in the city and the deserters who had deserted to the king of Babylon, together with the rest of the multitude, Nebuzaradan the captain of the guard carried into exile. But the captain of the guard left some of the poorest of the land to be vinedressers and plowmen.

And the pillars of bronze that were in the house of the LORD, and the stands and the bronze sea that were in the house of the LORD, the Chaldeans broke in pieces and carried the bronze to Babylon. And they took away the pots and the shovels and the snuffers and the dishes for incense and all the vessels of bronze used in the temple service, the fire pans also and the bowls. What was of gold the captain of the guard took away as gold, and what was of silver, as silver. As for the two pillars, the one sea, and the stands that Solomon had made for the house of the LORD, the bronze of all these vessels was beyond weight. The height of the one pillar was eighteen cubits, and on it was a capital of bronze. The height of the capital was three cubits. A latticework and pomegranates, all of bronze, were all around the capital. And the second pillar had the same, with the latticework.

And the captain of the guard took Seraiah the chief priest and Zephaniah the second priest and the three keepers of the threshold; and from the city he took an officer who had been in command of the men of war, and five men of the king's council who were found in the city; and the secretary of the commander of the army, who mustered the people of the land; and sixty men of the people of the land, who were found in the city. And Nebuzaradan the captain of the guard took them and brought them to the king of Babylon at Riblah. And the king of Babylon struck them down and put them to death at Riblah in the land of Hamath. So Judah was taken into exile out of its land.

Exiles Return and Rebuild the Temple

Israel was in exile in Babylon, away from its land, for about seventy years. After several decades God raised up a Persian king named Cyrus to defeat the Babylonians and send God's people back home.

The small number of Israelites who returned to the land was like a new Israel. But these exiles returned as a broken people to a broken land with a broken-down temple. In this next reading we see them begin to rebuild the temple. However, we also see many older Israelites weep when the temple is completed. They weep because this temple is not even close to the beauty of the previous one. They are back in the land, but they are still discouraged.

EZRA 3:1–13

When the seventh month came, and the children of Israel were in the towns, the people gathered as one man to Jerusalem. Then arose Jeshua the son of Jozadak, with his fellow priests, and Zerubbabel the son of Shealtiel with his kinsmen, and they built the altar of the God of Israel, to offer burnt offerings on it, as it is written in the Law of Moses the man of God. They set the altar in its place, for fear was on them because of the peoples of the lands, and they offered burnt offerings on it to the LORD, burnt offerings morning and evening. And they kept the Feast of Booths, as it is written, and offered the daily burnt offerings by number according to the rule, as each day required, and after that the regular burnt offerings, the offerings at the new moon and at all the appointed feasts of the LORD, and the offerings of everyone who made a freewill offering to the LORD. From the first day of the seventh month they began to offer burnt offerings to the LORD. But the foundation of the temple of the LORD was not yet laid. So they gave money to the masons and the carpenters, and food, drink, and oil to the Sidonians and the Tyrians to bring cedar trees from Lebanon to the sea, to Joppa, according to the grant that they had from Cyrus king of Persia.

Now in the second year after their coming to the house of God at Jerusalem, in the second month, Zerubbabel the son of Shealtiel and Jeshua the son of Jozadak made a beginning, together with the rest of their kinsmen, the priests and the Levites and all who had come to Jerusalem from the captivity. They appointed the Levites, from twenty years old and upward, to supervise the work of the house of the LORD. And Jeshua with his sons and his brothers, and Kadmiel and his sons, the sons of Judah, together supervised the workmen in the house of God, along with the sons of Henadad and the Levites, their sons and brothers.

And when the builders laid the foundation of the temple of the LORD, the priests in their vestments came forward with trumpets, and the Levites, the sons of Asaph, with cymbals, to praise the LORD, according to the directions of David king of Israel. And they sang responsively, praising and giving thanks to the LORD,

"For he is good,
for his steadfast love endures forever toward Israel."

And all the people shouted with a great shout when they praised the LORD, because the foundation of the house of the LORD was laid. But many of the priests and Levites and heads of fathers' houses, old men who had seen the first house, wept with a loud voice when they saw the foundation of this house being laid, though many shouted aloud for joy, so that the people could not distinguish the sound of the joyful shout from the sound of the people's weeping, for the people shouted with a great shout, and the sound was heard far away.

Israel Recommits to Obey God

The first group of Israelites who returned to the land began to rebuild the temple. Eventually a second group came, which included a priest named Ezra. By the time he arrived, God's people were once again failing to trust the Lord. Israel's unfaithfulness troubled Ezra. He recognized that God was graciously restoring the nation, yet Israel still refused to trust him.

Another leader named Nehemiah eventually returned to rebuild Jerusalem's walls. In the following account he leads the people in prayer. In this prayer we hear them acknowledge that they have sinned throughout their time as a nation. This explains why they have not experienced all the blessings God had promised. They feel like slaves in their own land, and the deepest reason for this is because they are still slaves to sin. They need God to give them new hearts so that they can truly turn to him.

NEHEMIAH 9:1–38

Now on the twenty-fourth day of this month the people of Israel were assembled with fasting and in sackcloth, and with earth on their heads. And the Israelites separated themselves from all foreigners and stood and confessed their sins and the iniquities of their fathers. And they stood up in their place and read from the Book of the Law of the LORD their God for a quarter of the day; for another quarter of it they made confession and worshiped the LORD their God. On the stairs of the Levites stood Jeshua, Bani, Kadmiel, Shebaniah, Bunni, Sherebiah, Bani, and Chenani; and they cried with a loud voice to the LORD their God. Then the Levites, Jeshua, Kadmiel, Bani, Hashabneiah, Sherebiah, Hodiah, Shebaniah, and Pethahiah, said, "Stand up and bless the LORD your God from everlasting to everlasting. Blessed be your glorious name, which is exalted above all blessing and praise.

"You are the LORD, you alone. You have made heaven, the heaven of heavens, with all their host, the earth and all that is on it, the seas and all that is in them; and you preserve all of them; and the host of heaven worships you. You are the LORD, the God who chose Abram and brought him out of Ur of the Chaldeans and gave him the name Abraham. You found his heart faithful before you, and made with him the covenant to give to his offspring the land of the Canaanite, the Hittite, the Amorite, the Perizzite, the Jebusite, and the Girgashite. And you have kept your promise, for you are righteous.

"And you saw the affliction of our fathers in Egypt and heard their cry at the Red Sea, and performed signs and wonders against Pharaoh and all his servants and all the people of his land, for you knew that they acted arrogantly against our fathers. And you made a name for yourself, as it is to this day. And you divided the sea before them, so that they went through the midst of the sea on dry land, and you cast their pursuers into the depths, as a stone into mighty waters. By a pillar of cloud you led them in the day, and by a pillar of fire in the night to light for them the way in which they should go. You came down on Mount Sinai and spoke with them from heaven and gave them right rules and true laws, good statutes and commandments, and you made known to them your holy Sabbath and commanded them commandments and statutes and a law by Moses your servant. You gave them bread from heaven for their hunger and brought water for them out of the rock for their thirst, and you told them to go in to possess the land that you had sworn to give them.

"But they and our fathers acted presumptuously and stiffened their neck and did not obey your commandments. They refused to obey and were not mindful of the wonders that you performed among them, but they stiffened their neck and appointed a leader to return to their slavery in Egypt. But you are a God ready to forgive, gracious and merciful, slow to anger and abounding in steadfast love, and did not forsake them. Even when they had made for themselves a golden calf and said, 'This is your God who brought you up out of Egypt,' and had committed great blasphemies, you in your great mercies did not forsake them in the wilderness. The pillar of cloud to lead them in the way did not depart from them by day, nor the pillar of fire by night to light for them the way by which they should go. You gave your good Spirit to instruct them and did not withhold your manna from their mouth and gave them water for their thirst. Forty years you sustained them in the wilderness, and they lacked nothing. Their clothes did not wear out and their feet did not swell.

"And you gave them kingdoms and peoples and allotted to them every corner. So they took possession of the land of Sihon king of Heshbon and the land of Og king of Bashan. You multiplied their children as the stars of heaven, and you brought them into the land that you had told their fathers to enter and possess. So the descendants went in and possessed the land, and you subdued before them the inhabitants of the land, the Canaanites, and gave them into their hand, with their kings and the peoples of the land, that they might do with them as they would. And they captured fortified cities and a rich land, and took possession of houses full of all good things, cisterns already hewn, vineyards, olive orchards and fruit trees in abundance. So they ate and were filled and became fat and delighted themselves in your great goodness.

"Nevertheless, they were disobedient and rebelled against you and cast your law behind their back and killed your prophets, who had warned them in order to turn them back to you, and they committed great blasphemies. Therefore you gave them into the hand of their enemies, who made them suffer. And in the time of their suffering they cried out to you and you heard them from heaven, and according to your great mercies you gave them saviors who saved them from the hand of their enemies. But after they had rest they did evil again before you, and you abandoned them to the hand of their enemies, so that they had dominion over them. Yet when they turned and cried to you, you heard from heaven, and many times you delivered them according to your mercies. And you warned them in order to turn them back to your law. Yet they acted presumptuously and did not obey your commandments, but sinned against your rules, which if a person does them, he shall live by them, and they turned a stubborn shoulder and stiffened their neck and would not obey. Many years you bore with them and warned them by your Spirit through your prophets. Yet they would not give ear. Therefore you gave them into the hand of the peoples of the lands. Nevertheless, in your great mercies you did not make an end of them or forsake them, for you are a gracious and merciful God.

"Now, therefore, our God, the great, the mighty, and the awesome God, who keeps covenant and steadfast love, let not all the hardship seem little to you that has come upon us, upon our kings, our princes, our priests, our prophets, our fathers, and all your people, since the time of the kings of Assyria until this day. Yet you have been righteous in all that has come upon us, for you have dealt faithfully and we have acted wickedly. Our kings, our princes, our priests, and our fathers have not kept your law or paid attention to your commandments and your warnings that you gave them. Even in their own kingdom, and amid your great goodness that you gave them, and in the large and rich land that you set before them, they did not serve you or turn from their wicked works. Behold, we are slaves this day; in the land that you gave to our fathers to enjoy its fruit and its good gifts, behold, we are slaves. And its rich yield goes to the kings whom you have set over us because of our sins. They rule over our bodies and over our livestock as they please, and we are in great distress.

"Because of all this we make a firm covenant in writing; on the sealed document are the names of our princes, our Levites, and our priests."

Part 5

THE HOPE OF
RESTORATION

The Hope of a New Exodus

God sent Israel many prophets who gave warnings and hope for the future. The prophet Isaiah showed that Israel's past exodus deliverance was a pattern for a greater redemption to come through Jesus. In the first exodus God freed Israel from slavery to Egypt. But through Isaiah God promised a greater deliverance, this time from slavery to sin and death. And he would restore not only Israel but people from all nations.

At the center of this salvation was God's "servant." This was a title for Israel, but it referred also to a single person: one ideal Israelite. The servant would live the faithful life we failed to live, die as a sacrifice for sins, and then rise again in victory. This servant would bring salvation to believing Israelites, and then to all nations. Jesus eventually came as this servant to deliver us from sin and death. And he did so as Isaiah promised: through his faithful life, his death in our place, and his resurrection.

ISAIAH 53:1–12

Who has believed what he has heard from us?
And to whom has the arm of the Lord been revealed?
For he grew up before him like a young plant,
    and like a root out of dry ground;
he had no form or majesty that we should look at him,
    and no beauty that we should desire him.
He was despised and rejected by men,
    a man of sorrows and acquainted with grief;
and as one from whom men hide their faces
    he was despised, and we esteemed him not.

Surely he has borne our griefs
    and carried our sorrows;
yet we esteemed him stricken,
    smitten by God, and afflicted.
But he was pierced for our transgressions;
    he was crushed for our iniquities;
upon him was the chastisement that brought us peace,
    and with his wounds we are healed.
All we like sheep have gone astray;
    we have turned — every one — to his own way;

and the LORD has laid on him
    the iniquity of us all.

He was oppressed, and he was afflicted,
    yet he opened not his mouth;
like a lamb that is led to the slaughter,
    and like a sheep that before its shearers is silent,
    so he opened not his mouth.
By oppression and judgment he was taken away;
    and as for his generation, who considered
that he was cut off out of the land of the living,
    stricken for the transgression of my people?
And they made his grave with the wicked
    and with a rich man in his death,
although he had done no violence,
    and there was no deceit in his mouth.

Yet it was the will of the LORD to crush him;
    he has put him to grief;
when his soul makes an offering for guilt,
    he shall see his offspring; he shall prolong his
        days;
the will of the LORD shall prosper in his hand.
Out of the anguish of his soul he shall see and be
        satisfied;
by his knowledge shall the righteous one, my servant,
    make many to be accounted righteous,
    and he shall bear their iniquities.

Therefore I will divide him a portion with the many,
  and he shall divide the spoil with the strong,
because he poured out his soul to death
  and was numbered with the transgressors;
yet he bore the sin of many,
  and makes intercession for the transgressors.

The Hope of a New Creation

Isaiah shows that God's plans for redemption were not just for Israel but for all nations. And his plan was to renew not just Israel but the whole planet. He would make the world like Eden again, but even better.

The following text from Isaiah shows God's incredible promise to return to his people and renew creation. And the most shocking part of it all was the Lord's heartfelt happiness about this plan. He will rejoice — *rejoice!* — over his people. He honors the humble. He delights in those who are sad about their sins and yet trust in him. And he gladly moves history toward an Eden-like new creation, where his people will live with him forever.

ISAIAH 65:1–25

I was ready to be sought by those who did not ask
    for me;
    I was ready to be found by those who did not
    seek me.
I said, "Here I am, here I am,"
    to a nation that was not called by my name.
I spread out my hands all the day
    to a rebellious people,
who walk in a way that is not good,
    following their own devices;
a people who provoke me
    to my face continually,
sacrificing in gardens
    and making offerings on bricks;
who sit in tombs,
    and spend the night in secret places;
who eat pig's flesh,
    and broth of tainted meat is in their vessels;
who say, "Keep to yourself,
    do not come near me, for I am too holy for you."

These are a smoke in my nostrils,
  a fire that burns all the day.
Behold, it is written before me:
   "I will not keep silent, but I will repay;
I will indeed repay into their lap
    both your iniquities and your fathers' iniquities
      together,
                    says the LORD;
because they made offerings on the mountains
    and insulted me on the hills,
I will measure into their lap
    payment for their former deeds."

Thus says the LORD:
"As the new wine is found in the cluster,
    and they say, 'Do not destroy it,
    for there is a blessing in it,'
so I will do for my servants' sake,
    and not destroy them all.
I will bring forth offspring from Jacob,
    and from Judah possessors of my mountains;
my chosen shall possess it,
    and my servants shall dwell there.
Sharon shall become a pasture for flocks,
    and the Valley of Achor a place for herds to lie
      down,
    for my people who have sought me.

But you who forsake the LORD,
    who forget my holy mountain,
who set a table for Fortune
    and fill cups of mixed wine for Destiny,
I will destine you to the sword,
    and all of you shall bow down to the slaughter,
because, when I called, you did not answer;
    when I spoke, you did not listen,
but you did what was evil in my eyes
    and chose what I did not delight in."

Therefore thus says the Lord GOD:
"Behold, my servants shall eat,
    but you shall be hungry;
behold, my servants shall drink,
    but you shall be thirsty;
behold, my servants shall rejoice,
    but you shall be put to shame;
behold, my servants shall sing for gladness of heart,
    but you shall cry out for pain of heart
    and shall wail for breaking of spirit.
You shall leave your name to my chosen for a curse,
    and the Lord GOD will put you to death,
    but his servants he will call by another name,
so that he who blesses himself in the land
    shall bless himself by the God of truth,

and he who takes an oath in the land
    shall swear by the God of truth;
because the former troubles are forgotten
    and are hidden from my eyes.

"For behold, I create new heavens
    and a new earth,
and the former things shall not be remembered
    or come into mind.
But be glad and rejoice forever
    in that which I create;
for behold, I create Jerusalem to be a joy,
    and her people to be a gladness.
I will rejoice in Jerusalem
    and be glad in my people;
no more shall be heard in it the sound of weeping
    and the cry of distress.
No more shall there be in it
    an infant who lives but a few days,
    or an old man who does not fill out his days,
for the young man shall die a hundred years old,
    and the sinner a hundred years old shall be accursed.
They shall build houses and inhabit them;
    they shall plant vineyards and eat their fruit.
They shall not build and another inhabit;
    they shall not plant and another eat;

for like the days of a tree shall the days of my people be,
    and my chosen shall long enjoy the work of their
        hands.
They shall not labor in vain
    or bear children for calamity,
for they shall be the offspring of the blessed of the LORD,
    and their descendants with them.
Before they call I will answer;
    while they are yet speaking I will hear.
The wolf and the lamb shall graze together;
    the lion shall eat straw like the ox,
    and dust shall be the serpent's food.
They shall not hurt or destroy
    in all my holy mountain,"

                                        says the LORD.

The Hope of a New Covenant

God chose his people, Israel, saved them from Egypt, and entered into a covenant relationship with them. Yet Israel broke this covenant relationship from the start by failing to love, trust, and obey him.

But then God offered a wonderful promise through the prophet Jeremiah: a new and better covenant. The Israelites could not keep the first covenant because their hearts were hard and unloving. But now God promised to forgive them and write his law on their hearts. He would make sure that everyone in the new covenant would know him and walk in his ways. Everyone in this new covenant would have full forgiveness, soft hearts, and the Holy Spirit's transforming power. People would now enjoy a permanent relationship with the Lord. Jesus eventually brought this new covenant through his life, death, resurrection, and sending of the Spirit.

JEREMIAH 31:1–40

"At that time, declares the LORD, I will be the God of all the clans of Israel, and they shall be my people."

Thus says the LORD:
"The people who survived the sword
    found grace in the wilderness;
when Israel sought for rest,
    the LORD appeared to him from far away.
I have loved you with an everlasting love;
    therefore I have continued my faithfulness to you.
Again I will build you, and you shall be built,
    O virgin Israel!
Again you shall adorn yourself with tambourines
    and shall go forth in the dance of the merrymakers.
Again you shall plant vineyards
    on the mountains of Samaria;
the planters shall plant
    and shall enjoy the fruit.
For there shall be a day when watchmen will call
    in the hill country of Ephraim:
'Arise, and let us go up to Zion,
    to the LORD our God.'"

For thus says the LORD:
"Sing aloud with gladness for Jacob,
and raise shouts for the chief of the nations;
proclaim, give praise, and say,
'O LORD, save your people,
the remnant of Israel.'
Behold, I will bring them from the north country
and gather them from the farthest parts of the
earth,
among them the blind and the lame,
the pregnant woman and she who is in labor,
together;
a great company, they shall return here.
With weeping they shall come,
and with pleas for mercy I will lead them back,
I will make them walk by brooks of water,
in a straight path in which they shall not stumble,
for I am a father to Israel,
and Ephraim is my firstborn.

"Hear the word of the LORD, O nations,
and declare it in the coastlands far away;
say, 'He who scattered Israel will gather him,
and will keep him as a shepherd keeps his flock.'
For the LORD has ransomed Jacob
and has redeemed him from hands too strong for
him.

They shall come and sing aloud on the height of Zion,
  and they shall be radiant over the goodness of the
    LORD,
over the grain, the wine, and the oil,
  and over the young of the flock and the herd;
their life shall be like a watered garden,
  and they shall languish no more.
Then shall the young women rejoice in the dance,
  and the young men and the old shall be merry.
I will turn their mourning into joy;
  I will comfort them, and give them gladness for
    sorrow.
I will feast the soul of the priests with abundance,
  and my people shall be satisfied with my goodness,
                          declares the LORD."

Thus says the LORD:
"A voice is heard in Ramah,
  lamentation and bitter weeping.
Rachel is weeping for her children;
  she refuses to be comforted for her children,
  because they are no more."

Thus says the LORD:
"Keep your voice from weeping,
  and your eyes from tears,
for there is a reward for your work,
                          declares the LORD,

and they shall come back from the land of the
    enemy.
There is hope for your future,
                   declares the LORD,
and your children shall come back to their own
    country.
I have heard Ephraim grieving,
'You have disciplined me, and I was disciplined,
    like an untrained calf;
bring me back that I may be restored,
    for you are the LORD my God.
For after I had turned away, I relented,
    and after I was instructed, I struck my thigh;
I was ashamed, and I was confounded,
    because I bore the disgrace of my youth.'
Is Ephraim my dear son?
    Is he my darling child?
For as often as I speak against him,
    I do remember him still.
Therefore my heart yearns for him;
    I will surely have mercy on him,
                   declares the LORD.

"Set up road markers for yourself;
    make yourself guideposts;
consider well the highway,
    the road by which you went.

Return, O virgin Israel,

   return to these your cities.

How long will you waver,

   O faithless daughter?

For the LORD has created a new thing on the earth:

   a woman encircles a man."

Thus says the LORD of hosts, the God of Israel: "Once more they shall use these words in the land of Judah and in its cities, when I restore their fortunes:

   "'The LORD bless you, O habitation of righteousness,

      O holy hill!'

And Judah and all its cities shall dwell there together, and the farmers and those who wander with their flocks. For I will satisfy the weary soul, and every languishing soul I will replenish."

At this I awoke and looked, and my sleep was pleasant to me.

"Behold, the days are coming, declares the LORD, when I will sow the house of Israel and the house of Judah with the seed of man and the seed of beast. And it shall come to pass that as I have watched over them to pluck up and break down, to overthrow, destroy, and bring harm, so I will watch over them to build and to plant, declares the LORD. In those days they shall no longer say:

   "'The fathers have eaten sour grapes,

      and the children's teeth are set on edge.'

But everyone shall die for his own iniquity. Each man who eats sour grapes, his teeth shall be set on edge.

"Behold, the days are coming, declares the LORD, when I will make a new covenant with the house of Israel and the house of Judah, not like the covenant that I made with their fathers on the day when I took them by the hand to bring them out of the land of Egypt, my covenant that they broke, though I was their husband, declares the LORD. For this is the covenant that I will make with the house of Israel after those days, declares the LORD: I will put my law within them, and I will write it on their hearts. And I will be their God, and they shall be my people. And no longer shall each one teach his neighbor and each his brother, saying, 'Know the LORD,' for they shall all know me, from the least of them to the greatest, declares the LORD. For I will forgive their iniquity, and I will remember their sin no more."

> Thus says the LORD,
>   who gives the sun for light by day
>   and the fixed order of the moon and the stars for
>   light by night,
>   who stirs up the sea so that its waves roar—
>   the LORD of hosts is his name:
> "If this fixed order departs
>   from before me, declares the LORD,
>   then shall the offspring of Israel cease
>   from being a nation before me forever."

Thus says the LORD:
"If the heavens above can be measured,
 and the foundations of the earth below can be
  explored,
then I will cast off all the offspring of Israel
 for all that they have done,
        declares the LORD."

"Behold, the days are coming, declares the LORD, when the city shall be rebuilt for the LORD from the Tower of Hananel to the Corner Gate. And the measuring line shall go out farther, straight to the hill Gareb, and shall then turn to Goah. The whole valley of the dead bodies and the ashes, and all the fields as far as the brook Kidron, to the corner of the Horse Gate toward the east, shall be sacred to the LORD. It shall not be plucked up or overthrown anymore forever."

The Hope of New Life

Through the prophets Isaiah and Jeremiah God promised a new exodus, a new creation, and a new covenant. Ezekiel added the promise of new life.

Israel needed this new life. Its exile from the land was itself like the death of the nation. Most of the people were also spiritually dead. They were separated from God, the source of life. Like the rest of humanity, they needed new hearts. They needed a new spirit. They needed spiritual life. And they were utterly incapable of finding these things on their own. So God promised what only he could do: to breathe new life into them and raise them from the dead. Only a God of unlimited power *could* do this, and only a God of infinite grace *would* do this. The prophets show that history is moving toward a day in which God's people will be resurrected and renewed.

EZEKIEL 37:1–28

T he hand of the LORD was upon me, and he brought me out in the Spirit of the LORD and set me down in the middle of the valley; it was full of bones. And he led me around among them, and behold, there were very many on the surface of the valley, and behold, they were very dry. And he said to me, "Son of man, can these bones live?" And I answered, "O Lord GOD, you know." Then he said to me, "Prophesy over these bones, and say to them, O dry bones, hear the word of the LORD. Thus says the Lord GOD to these bones: Behold, I will cause breath to enter you, and you shall live. And I will lay sinews upon you, and will cause flesh to come upon you, and cover you with skin, and put breath in you, and you shall live, and you shall know that I am the LORD."

So I prophesied as I was commanded. And as I prophesied, there was a sound, and behold, a rattling, and the bones came together, bone to its bone. And I looked, and behold, there were sinews on them, and flesh had come upon them, and skin had covered them. But there was no breath in them. Then he said to me, "Prophesy to the breath; prophesy, son of man, and say to the breath, Thus says the Lord GOD: Come from the four winds, O breath, and breathe on these slain, that they may live." So I prophesied as he commanded me, and the breath came into them, and they lived and stood on their feet, an exceedingly great army.

Then he said to me, "Son of man, these bones are the whole house of Israel. Behold, they say, 'Our bones are dried up, and our hope is lost; we are indeed cut off.' Therefore prophesy, and say to them, Thus says the Lord GOD: Behold, I will open your graves and raise you from your graves, O my people. And I will bring you into the land of Israel. And you shall know that I am the LORD, when I open your graves, and raise you from your graves, O my people. And I will put my Spirit within you, and you shall live, and I will place you in your own land. Then you shall know that I am the LORD; I have spoken, and I will do it, declares the LORD."

The word of the LORD came to me: "Son of man, take a stick and write on it, 'For Judah, and the people of Israel associated with him'; then take another stick and write on it, 'For Joseph (the stick of Ephraim) and all the house of Israel associated with him.' And join them one to another into one stick, that they may become one in your hand. And when your people say to you, 'Will you not tell us what you mean by these?' say to them, Thus says the Lord GOD: Behold, I am about to take the stick of Joseph (that is in the hand of Ephraim) and the tribes of Israel associated with him. And I will join with it the stick of Judah, and make them one stick, that they may be one in my hand. When the sticks on which you write are in your hand before their eyes, then say to them, Thus says the Lord GOD: Behold, I will take the people of Israel from the nations among which they have gone, and will gather them from all around, and bring them to their own land.

And I will make them one nation in the land, on the mountains of Israel. And one king shall be king over them all, and they shall be no longer two nations, and no longer divided into two kingdoms. They shall not defile themselves anymore with their idols and their detestable things, or with any of their transgressions. But I will save them from all the backslidings in which they have sinned, and will cleanse them; and they shall be my people, and I will be their God.

"My servant David shall be king over them, and they shall all have one shepherd. They shall walk in my rules and be careful to obey my statutes. They shall dwell in the land that I gave to my servant Jacob, where your fathers lived. They and their children and their children's children shall dwell there forever, and David my servant shall be their prince forever. I will make a covenant of peace with them. It shall be an everlasting covenant with them. And I will set them in their land and multiply them, and will set my sanctuary in their midst forevermore. My dwelling place shall be with them, and I will be their God, and they shall be my people. Then the nations will know that I am the LORD who sanctifies Israel, when my sanctuary is in their midst forevermore."

Part 6

THE DAWNING OF
THE KINGDOM

Jesus' Ministry Begins

The Old Testament story began with God's perfect kingdom in Eden. But after our first parents rejected God, the Lord promised to send a Savior to crush the head of the Serpent. This Savior would restore God's blessing to the world. God developed this promise through covenants with Noah, Abraham, Moses, and David. By the end of the Old Testament we are waiting for the Lord himself to come with his kingdom.

The Gospel of Mark announces that Jesus has come to fulfill these promises. He declares, "The time is fulfilled, and the kingdom of God is at hand; repent and believe in the gospel." Mark shows us that Jesus is truly God and truly human—we are invited to trust him, receive his forgiveness, and follow him.

MARK 1:1-45

T he beginning of the gospel of Jesus Christ, the Son of God. As it is written in Isaiah the prophet,

> "Behold, I send my messenger before your face,
>> who will prepare your way,
> the voice of one crying in the wilderness:
>> 'Prepare the way of the Lord,
>> make his paths straight,' "

John appeared, baptizing in the wilderness and proclaiming a baptism of repentance for the forgiveness of sins. And all the country of Judea and all Jerusalem were going out to him and were being baptized by him in the river Jordan, confessing their sins. Now John was clothed with camel's hair and wore a leather belt around his waist and ate locusts and wild honey. And he preached, saying, "After me comes he who is mightier than I, the strap of whose sandals I am not worthy to stoop down and untie. I have baptized you with water, but he will baptize you with the Holy Spirit."

In those days Jesus came from Nazareth of Galilee and was baptized by John in the Jordan. And when he came up out of the water, immediately he saw the heavens being torn open and the

Spirit descending on him like a dove. And a voice came from heaven, "You are my beloved Son; with you I am well pleased."

The Spirit immediately drove him out into the wilderness. And he was in the wilderness forty days, being tempted by Satan. And he was with the wild animals, and the angels were ministering to him.

Now after John was arrested, Jesus came into Galilee, proclaiming the gospel of God, and saying, "The time is fulfilled, and the kingdom of God is at hand; repent and believe in the gospel."

Passing alongside the Sea of Galilee, he saw Simon and Andrew the brother of Simon casting a net into the sea, for they were fishermen. And Jesus said to them, "Follow me, and I will make you become fishers of men." And immediately they left their nets and followed him. And going on a little farther, he saw James the son of Zebedee and John his brother, who were in their boat mending the nets. And immediately he called them, and they left their father Zebedee in the boat with the hired servants and followed him.

And they went into Capernaum, and immediately on the Sabbath he entered the synagogue and was teaching. And they were astonished at his teaching, for he taught them as one who had authority, and not as the scribes. And immediately there was in their synagogue a man with an unclean spirit. And he cried out, "What have you to do with us, Jesus of Nazareth? Have you come to destroy us? I know who you are—the Holy One of God." But Jesus rebuked him, saying, "Be silent, and come out of him!" And the unclean spirit, convulsing him and crying out with a loud voice, came out of him. And they were all amazed, so that they questioned among themselves, saying, "What is this? A new teaching with authority! He commands even the unclean spirits, and they obey him." And at once his fame spread everywhere throughout all the surrounding region of Galilee.

And immediately he left the synagogue and entered the house of Simon and Andrew, with James and John. Now Simon's mother-in-law lay ill with a fever, and immediately they told him about her. And he came and took her by the hand and lifted her up, and the fever left her, and she began to serve them.

That evening at sundown they brought to him all who were sick or oppressed by demons. And the whole city was gathered together at the door. And he healed many who were sick with various diseases, and cast out many demons. And he would not permit the demons to speak, because they knew him.

And rising very early in the morning, while it was still dark, he departed and went out to a desolate place, and there he prayed. And Simon and those who were with him searched for him, and they found him and said to him, "Everyone is looking for you." And he said to them, "Let us go on to the next towns, that I may preach there also, for that is why I came out." And he went throughout all Galilee, preaching in their synagogues and casting out demons.

And a leper came to him, imploring him, and kneeling said to him, "If you will, you can make me clean." Moved with pity, he stretched out his hand and touched him and said to him, "I will; be clean." And immediately the leprosy left him, and he was made clean. And Jesus sternly charged him and sent him away at once, and said to him, "See that you say nothing to anyone, but go, show yourself to the priest and offer for your cleansing what Moses commanded, for a proof to them." But he went out and began to talk freely about it, and to spread the news, so that Jesus could no longer openly enter a town, but was out in desolate places, and people were coming to him from every quarter.

Jesus' Ministry Continues

Mark shows us who Jesus is and how God's kingdom comes into the world through him. We see him undo the bad effects of the curse — he forgives sins and heals sickness. He casts out demons and calms storms. He welcomes the lonely and befriends sinners. This is a preview of what it will look like when he comes again to establish his kingdom fully and forever. Jesus' kingdom is already and not yet here — it has come into the world and is growing but is not yet here in its fullness.

Jesus eventually asks his disciples the question he asks every one of us: "Who do you say that I am?" As we read the following text, we must conclude that Jesus either is lying, is crazy, or is who he says he is: the Christ, the Son of God, the King we have been awaiting. He is God himself, who has come to rescue us and to restore all things.

MARK 8:1-38

In those days, when again a great crowd had gathered, and they had nothing to eat, he called his disciples to him and said to them, "I have compassion on the crowd, because they have been with me now three days and have nothing to eat. And if I send them away hungry to their homes, they will faint on the way. And some of them have come from far away." And his disciples answered him, "How can one feed these people with bread here in this desolate place?" And he asked them, "How many loaves do you have?" They said, "Seven." And he directed the crowd to sit down on the ground. And he took the seven loaves, and having given thanks, he broke them and gave them to his disciples to set before the people; and they set them before the crowd. And they had a few small fish. And having blessed them, he said that these also should be set before them. And they ate and were satisfied. And they took up the broken pieces left over, seven baskets full. And there were about four thousand people. And he sent them away. And immediately he got into the boat with his disciples and went to the district of Dalmanutha.

The Pharisees came and began to argue with him, seeking from him a sign from heaven to test him. And he sighed deeply in his spirit and said, "Why does this generation seek a sign?

Truly, I say to you, no sign will be given to this generation." And he left them, got into the boat again, and went to the other side.

Now they had forgotten to bring bread, and they had only one loaf with them in the boat. And he cautioned them, saying, "Watch out; beware of the leaven of the Pharisees and the leaven of Herod." And they began discussing with one another the fact that they had no bread. And Jesus, aware of this, said to them, "Why are you discussing the fact that you have no bread? Do you not yet perceive or understand? Are your hearts hardened? Having eyes do you not see, and having ears do you not hear? And do you not remember? When I broke the five loaves for the five thousand, how many baskets full of broken pieces did you take up?" They said to him, "Twelve." "And the seven for the four thousand, how many baskets full of broken pieces did you take up?" And they said to him, "Seven." And he said to them, "Do you not yet understand?"

And they came to Bethsaida. And some people brought to him a blind man and begged him to touch him. And he took the blind man by the hand and led him out of the village, and when he had spit on his eyes and laid his hands on him, he asked him, "Do you see anything?" And he looked up and said, "I see people, but they look like trees, walking." Then Jesus laid his hands on his eyes again; and he opened his eyes, his sight was restored, and he saw everything clearly. And he sent him to his home, saying, "Do not even enter the village."

And Jesus went on with his disciples to the villages of Caesarea Philippi. And on the way he asked his disciples, "Who do people say that I am?" And they told him, "John the Baptist; and others say, Elijah; and others, one of the prophets." And he asked them, "But who do you say that I am?" Peter answered him, "You are the Christ." And he strictly charged them to tell no one about him.

And he began to teach them that the Son of Man must suffer many things and be rejected by the elders and the chief priests and the scribes and be killed, and after three days rise again. And he said this plainly. And Peter took him aside and began to rebuke him. But turning and seeing his disciples, he rebuked Peter and said, "Get behind me, Satan! For you are not setting your mind on the things of God, but on the things of man."

And calling the crowd to him with his disciples, he said to them, "If anyone would come after me, let him deny himself and take up his cross and follow me. For whoever would save his life will lose it, but whoever loses his life for my sake and the gospel's will save it. For what does it profit a man to gain the whole world and forfeit his soul? For what can a man give in return for his soul? For whoever is ashamed of me and of my words in this adulterous and sinful generation, of him will the Son of Man also be ashamed when he comes in the glory of his Father with the holy angels."

Jesus' Journey to Jerusalem

Many people think Jesus might be the true King, and they do not expect him to suffer. But Mark shows that Jesus is the prophet Isaiah's promised servant. Jesus must "give his life as a ransom for many." If anyone would follow him, one must admit the need for forgiveness. All must be reconciled to God. All need their King to die for their sins.

Jesus also taught his disciples what it means to follow him. In Jesus' kingdom we learn that true greatness is service. We learn to resist sin. We learn this when we recognize that the greatest treasure in life is Jesus.

A nd he left there and went to the region of Judea and beyond the Jordan, and crowds gathered to him again. And again, as was his custom, he taught them.

And Pharisees came up and in order to test him asked, "Is it lawful for a man to divorce his wife?" He answered them, "What did Moses command you?" They said, "Moses allowed a man to write a certificate of divorce and to send her away." And Jesus said to them, "Because of your hardness of heart he wrote you this commandment. But from the beginning of creation, 'God made them male and female.' 'Therefore a man shall leave his father and mother and hold fast to his wife, and the two shall become one flesh.' So they are no longer two but one flesh. What therefore God has joined together, let not man separate."

And in the house the disciples asked him again about this matter. And he said to them, "Whoever divorces his wife and marries another commits adultery against her, and if she divorces her husband and marries another, she commits adultery."

And they were bringing children to him that he might touch them, and the disciples rebuked them. But when Jesus saw it, he was indignant and said to them, "Let the children come to me; do not hinder them, for to such belongs the kingdom of God. Truly,

I say to you, whoever does not receive the kingdom of God like a child shall not enter it." And he took them in his arms and blessed them, laying his hands on them.

And as he was setting out on his journey, a man ran up and knelt before him and asked him, "Good Teacher, what must I do to inherit eternal life?" And Jesus said to him, "Why do you call me good? No one is good except God alone. You know the commandments: 'Do not murder, Do not commit adultery, Do not steal, Do not bear false witness, Do not defraud, Honor your father and mother.'" And he said to him, "Teacher, all these I have kept from my youth." And Jesus, looking at him, loved him, and said to him, "You lack one thing: go, sell all that you have and give to the poor, and you will have treasure in heaven; and come, follow me." Disheartened by the saying, he went away sorrowful, for he had great possessions.

And Jesus looked around and said to his disciples, "How difficult it will be for those who have wealth to enter the kingdom of God!" And the disciples were amazed at his words. But Jesus said to them again, "Children, how difficult it is to enter the kingdom of God! It is easier for a camel to go through the eye of a needle than for a rich person to enter the kingdom of God." And they were exceedingly astonished, and said to him, "Then who can be saved?" Jesus looked at them and said, "With man it is impossible, but not with God. For all things are possible with God." Peter began to say to him, "See, we have left everything and followed you." Jesus said, "Truly, I say to you, there is no one who has left house or brothers or sisters or mother or father or children or lands, for my sake and for the gospel, who will not receive a hundredfold now in this time, houses and brothers and sisters and mothers and children and lands, with persecutions, and in the age to come eternal life. But many who are first will be last, and the last first."

And they were on the road, going up to Jerusalem, and Jesus was walking ahead of them. And they were amazed, and those who followed were afraid. And taking the twelve again, he began to tell them what was to happen to him, saying, "See, we are going up to Jerusalem, and the Son of Man will be delivered over to the chief priests and the scribes, and they will condemn him to death and deliver him over to the Gentiles. And they will mock him and spit on him, and flog him and kill him. And after three days he will rise."

And James and John, the sons of Zebedee, came up to him and said to him, "Teacher, we want you to do for us whatever we ask of you." And he said to them, "What do you want me to do for you?" And they said to him, "Grant us to sit, one at your right hand and one at your left, in your glory." Jesus said to them, "You do not know what you are asking. Are you able to drink the cup that I drink, or to be baptized with the baptism with which I am baptized?" And they said to him, "We are able." And Jesus said to them, "The cup that I drink you will drink, and with the baptism with which I am baptized, you will be baptized, but to sit at my right hand or at my left is not mine to grant, but it is for those for whom it has been prepared." And when the ten heard it, they began to be indignant at James and John. And Jesus called them to him and said to them, "You know that those who are considered rulers of the Gentiles lord it over them, and their great ones exercise authority over them. But it shall not be so among you. But whoever would be great among you must be your servant, and whoever would be first among you must be slave of all. For even the Son of Man came not to be served but to serve, and to give his life as a ransom for many."

And they came to Jericho. And as he was leaving Jericho with his disciples and a great crowd, Bartimaeus, a blind beggar, the son of Timaeus, was sitting by the roadside. And when he heard that it was Jesus of Nazareth, he began to cry out and say, "Jesus, Son of David, have mercy on me!" And many rebuked him, telling him to be silent. But he cried out all the more, "Son of David, have mercy on me!" And Jesus stopped and said, "Call him." And they called the blind man, saying to him, "Take heart. Get up; he is calling you." And throwing off his cloak, he sprang up and came to Jesus. And Jesus said to him, "What do you want me to do for you?" And the blind man said to him, "Rabbi, let me recover my sight." And Jesus said to him, "Go your way; your faith has made you well." And immediately he recovered his sight and followed him on the way.

Jesus' Death and Resurrection

Mark carefully records Jesus' last hours, death, and resurrection. He emphasizes two truths: that these things really did happen in history and that they really do matter for us today. As with the sacrifices in the Old Testament, Jesus gave his life as the ultimate sacrifice. He was punished for the sins for which we deserved to die. He was cast out of God's presence so that we could be welcomed there. He was punished so that we could be accepted. He was judged so that we could be forgiven.

And then he rose in victory—the very first one to rise from the dead never to die again. When Adam and Eve sinned, God said they would die, and death spread to all people. But the prophets also said that one day God would raise his people from the dead. With Jesus' resurrection, God has begun to do so. This is the dawn of a new day.

And as soon as it was morning, the chief priests held a consultation with the elders and scribes and the whole council. And they bound Jesus and led him away and delivered him over to Pilate. And Pilate asked him, "Are you the King of the Jews?" And he answered him, "You have said so." And the chief priests accused him of many things. And Pilate again asked him, "Have you no answer to make? See how many charges they bring against you." But Jesus made no further answer, so that Pilate was amazed.

Now at the feast he used to release for them one prisoner for whom they asked. And among the rebels in prison, who had committed murder in the insurrection, there was a man called Barabbas. And the crowd came up and began to ask Pilate to do as he usually did for them. And he answered them, saying, "Do you want me to release for you the King of the Jews?" For he perceived that it was out of envy that the chief priests had delivered him up. But the chief priests stirred up the crowd to have him release for them Barabbas instead. And Pilate again said to them, "Then what shall I do with the man you call the King of the Jews?" And they cried out again, "Crucify him." And Pilate said to them, "Why? What evil has he done?" But they shouted all the more, "Crucify him." So Pilate, wishing to satisfy the crowd, released for them Barabbas, and having scourged Jesus, he delivered him to be crucified.

And the soldiers led him away inside the palace (that is, the governor's headquarters), and they called together the whole battalion. And they clothed him in a purple cloak, and twisting together a crown of thorns, they put it on him. And they began to salute him, "Hail, King of the Jews!" And they were striking his head with a reed and spitting on him and kneeling down in homage to him. And when they had mocked him, they stripped him of the purple cloak and put his own clothes on him. And they led him out to crucify him.

And they compelled a passerby, Simon of Cyrene, who was coming in from the country, the father of Alexander and Rufus, to carry his cross. And they brought him to the place called Golgotha (which means Place of a Skull). And they offered him wine mixed with myrrh, but he did not take it. And they crucified him and divided his garments among them, casting lots for them, to decide what each should take. And it was the third hour when they crucified him. And the inscription of the charge against him read, "The King of the Jews." And with him they crucified two robbers, one on his right and one on his left. And those who passed by derided him, wagging their heads and saying, "Aha! You who would destroy the temple and rebuild it in three days, save yourself, and come down from the cross!" So also the chief priests with the scribes mocked him to one another, saying, "He saved others; he cannot save himself. Let the Christ, the King of Israel, come down now from the cross that we may see and believe." Those who were crucified with him also reviled him.

And when the sixth hour had come, there was darkness over the whole land until the ninth hour. And at the ninth hour Jesus cried with a loud voice, "Eloi, Eloi, lema sabachthani?" which means, "My God, my God, why have you forsaken me?" And some of the bystanders hearing it said, "Behold, he is calling Elijah." And someone ran and filled a sponge with sour wine, put it on a reed and gave it to him to drink, saying, "Wait, let us see whether Elijah will come to take him down." And Jesus uttered a loud cry and breathed his last. And the curtain of the temple was torn in two, from top to bottom. And when the centurion, who stood facing him, saw that in this way he breathed his last, he said, "Truly this man was the Son of God!"

There were also women looking on from a distance, among whom were Mary Magdalene, and Mary the mother of James the younger and of Joses, and Salome. When he was in Galilee, they followed him and ministered to him, and there were also many other women who came up with him to Jerusalem.

And when evening had come, since it was the day of Preparation, that is, the day before the Sabbath, Joseph of Arimathea, a respected member of the council, who was also himself looking for the kingdom of God, took courage and went to Pilate and asked for the body of Jesus. Pilate was surprised to hear that he should have already died. And summoning the centurion, he asked him whether he was already dead. And when he learned from the centurion that he was dead, he granted the corpse to Joseph. And

Joseph bought a linen shroud, and taking him down, wrapped him in the linen shroud and laid him in a tomb that had been cut out of the rock. And he rolled a stone against the entrance of the tomb. Mary Magdalene and Mary the mother of Joses saw where he was laid.

When the Sabbath was past, Mary Magdalene, Mary the mother of James, and Salome bought spices, so that they might go and anoint him. And very early on the first day of the week, when the sun had risen, they went to the tomb. And they were saying to one another, "Who will roll away the stone for us from the entrance of the tomb?" And looking up, they saw that the stone had been rolled back—it was very large. And entering the tomb, they saw a young man sitting on the right side, dressed in a white robe, and they were alarmed. And he said to them, "Do not be alarmed. You seek Jesus of Nazareth, who was crucified. He has risen; he is not here. See the place where they laid him. But go, tell his disciples and Peter that he is going before you to Galilee. There you will see him, just as he told you." And they went out and fled from the tomb, for trembling and astonishment had seized them, and they said nothing to anyone, for they were afraid.

Part 7

THE GOSPEL SPREADS
AND ALL IS MADE NEW

The Church's Mission Begins

The risen Jesus is the world's true King, and he invites us to be forgiven and restored in order to know the true God. The book of Acts shows how his people now spread this good news to all nations through the power of the Holy Spirit. Jesus sent his disciples to be his witnesses "in Jerusalem and in all Judea and Samaria, and to the end of the earth" (Acts 1:8). That was the sequence Isaiah had promised: God would first restore Israel to himself, and then he would gather people from all nations.

Acts shows us how people find true happiness by knowing Jesus. They also find true friendship and community with other Christians. And they find a new purpose to tell others that Jesus is the King and everyone is welcomed to come to him through faith.

ACTS 2:1–47

When the day of Pentecost arrived, they were all together in one place. And suddenly there came from heaven a sound like a mighty rushing wind, and it filled the entire house where they were sitting. And divided tongues as of fire appeared to them and rested on each one of them. And they were all filled with the Holy Spirit and began to speak in other tongues as the Spirit gave them utterance.

Now there were dwelling in Jerusalem Jews, devout men from every nation under heaven. And at this sound the multitude came together, and they were bewildered, because each one was hearing them speak in his own language. And they were amazed and astonished, saying, "Are not all these who are speaking Galileans? And how is it that we hear, each of us in his own native language? Parthians and Medes and Elamites and residents of Mesopotamia, Judea and Cappadocia, Pontus and Asia, Phrygia and Pamphylia, Egypt and the parts of Libya belonging to Cyrene, and visitors from Rome, both Jews and proselytes, Cretans and Arabians—we hear them telling in our own tongues the mighty works of God." And all were amazed and perplexed, saying to one another, "What does this mean?" But others mocking said, "They are filled with new wine."

But Peter, standing with the eleven, lifted up his voice and addressed them: "Men of Judea and all who dwell in Jerusalem, let this be known to you, and give ear to my words. For these people are not drunk, as you suppose, since it is only the third hour of the day. But this is what was uttered through the prophet Joel:

> "'And in the last days it shall be, God declares,
>> that I will pour out my Spirit on all flesh,
>> and your sons and your daughters shall prophesy,
>>> and your young men shall see visions,
>>> and your old men shall dream dreams;
>> even on my male servants and female servants
>>> in those days I will pour out my Spirit, and they
>>>> shall prophesy.
>> And I will show wonders in the heavens above
>>> and signs on the earth below,
>>> blood, and fire, and vapor of smoke;
>> the sun shall be turned to darkness
>>> and the moon to blood,
>>> before the day of the Lord comes, the great and
>>>> magnificent day.
>> And it shall come to pass that everyone who calls
>>> upon the name of the Lord shall be saved.'

"Men of Israel, hear these words: Jesus of Nazareth, a man attested to you by God with mighty works and wonders and signs that God did through him in your midst, as you yourselves know—this Jesus, delivered up according to the definite plan and foreknowledge of God, you crucified and killed by the hands of lawless men. God raised him up, loosing the pangs of death, because it was not possible for him to be held by it. For David says concerning him,

> "'I saw the Lord always before me,
>> for he is at my right hand that I may not be shaken;
> therefore my heart was glad, and my tongue rejoiced;
>> my flesh also will dwell in hope.
> For you will not abandon my soul to Hades,
>> or let your Holy One see corruption.
> You have made known to me the paths of life;
>> you will make me full of gladness with your
>> presence.'

"Brothers, I may say to you with confidence about the patriarch David that he both died and was buried, and his tomb is with us to this day. Being therefore a prophet, and knowing that God had sworn with an oath to him that he would set one of his descendants on his throne, he foresaw and spoke about the resurrection of the Christ, that he was not abandoned to Hades, nor did his flesh see corruption. This Jesus God raised up, and of that we all are witnesses. Being therefore exalted at the right hand of God, and having received from the Father the promise of the Holy Spirit, he has poured out this that you yourselves are seeing and hearing. For David did not ascend into the heavens, but he himself says,

> " 'The Lord said to my Lord,
>
>   "Sit at my right hand,
>
>   until I make your enemies your footstool." '

Let all the house of Israel therefore know for certain that God has made him both Lord and Christ, this Jesus whom you crucified."

Now when they heard this they were cut to the heart, and said to Peter and the rest of the apostles, "Brothers, what shall we do?" And Peter said to them, "Repent and be baptized every one of you in the name of Jesus Christ for the forgiveness of your sins, and you will receive the gift of the Holy Spirit. For the promise is for you and for your children and for all who are far off, everyone whom the Lord our God calls to himself." And with many other words he bore witness and continued to exhort them, saying, "Save yourselves from this crooked generation." So those who received his word were baptized, and there were added that day about three thousand souls.

And they devoted themselves to the apostles' teaching and the fellowship, to the breaking of bread and the prayers. And awe came upon every soul, and many wonders and signs were being done through the apostles. And all who believed were together and had all things in common. And they were selling their possessions and belongings and distributing the proceeds to all, as any had need. And day by day, attending the temple together and breaking bread in their homes, they received their food with glad and generous hearts, praising God and having favor with all the people. And the Lord added to their number day by day those who were being saved.

The Church Multiplies in Jerusalem and Beyond

Jesus commissioned his disciples to go tell the world about him, but he also insisted they wait. They needed the power of the Spirit. Christians need the Spirit to give them courage to tell people about Jesus. And others need the Spirit to open their hearts so they might believe in Jesus.

Acts shows us what it looks like when the Spirit changes hearts so that people start following Jesus. The first Christians worshiped God and shared life in true community. They also lived with a new mission to tell people the good news about Jesus. Even when they suffered for being Christians, they had deep joy. The next part of Acts shows how the gospel continued to spread beyond Jerusalem.

But a man named Ananias, with his wife Sapphira, sold a piece of property, and with his wife's knowledge he kept back for himself some of the proceeds and brought only a part of it and laid it at the apostles' feet. But Peter said, "Ananias, why has Satan filled your heart to lie to the Holy Spirit and to keep back for yourself part of the proceeds of the land? While it remained unsold, did it not remain your own? And after it was sold, was it not at your disposal? Why is it that you have contrived this deed in your heart? You have not lied to man but to God." When Ananias heard these words, he fell down and breathed his last. And great fear came upon all who heard of it. The young men rose and wrapped him up and carried him out and buried him.

After an interval of about three hours his wife came in, not knowing what had happened. And Peter said to her, "Tell me whether you sold the land for so much." And she said, "Yes, for so much." But Peter said to her, "How is it that you have agreed together to test the Spirit of the Lord? Behold, the feet of those who have buried your husband are at the door, and they will carry you out." Immediately she fell down at his feet and breathed her last. When the young men came in they found her dead, and they carried her out and buried her beside her husband. And great fear came upon the whole church and upon all who heard of these things.

Now many signs and wonders were regularly done among the people by the hands of the apostles. And they were all together in Solomon's Portico. None of the rest dared join them, but the people held them in high esteem. And more than ever believers were added to the Lord, multitudes of both men and women, so that they even carried out the sick into the streets and laid them on cots and mats, that as Peter came by at least his shadow might fall on some of them. The people also gathered from the towns around Jerusalem, bringing the sick and those afflicted with unclean spirits, and they were all healed.

But the high priest rose up, and all who were with him (that is, the party of the Sadducees), and filled with jealousy they arrested the apostles and put them in the public prison. But during the night an angel of the Lord opened the prison doors and brought them out, and said, "Go and stand in the temple and speak to the people all the words of this Life." And when they heard this, they entered the temple at daybreak and began to teach.

Now when the high priest came, and those who were with him, they called together the council, all the senate of the people of Israel, and sent to the prison to have them brought. But when the officers came, they did not find them in the prison, so they returned and reported, "We found the prison securely locked and the guards standing at the doors, but when we opened them we found no one inside." Now when the captain of the temple and the chief priests heard these words, they were greatly perplexed about them, wondering what this would come to. And someone came and told them, "Look! The men whom you put in prison are standing in the temple and teaching the people." Then the captain with the officers went and brought them, but not by force, for they were afraid of being stoned by the people.

And when they had brought them, they set them before the council. And the high priest questioned them, saying, "We strictly charged you not to teach in this name, yet here you have filled Jerusalem with your teaching, and you intend to bring this man's blood upon us." But Peter and the apostles answered, "We must obey God rather than men. The God of our fathers raised Jesus, whom you killed by hanging him on a tree. God exalted him at his right hand as Leader and Savior, to give repentance to Israel and forgiveness of sins. And we are witnesses to these things, and so is the Holy Spirit, whom God has given to those who obey him."

When they heard this, they were enraged and wanted to kill them. But a Pharisee in the council named Gamaliel, a teacher of the law held in honor by all the people, stood up and gave orders to put the men outside for a little while. And he said to them, "Men of Israel, take care what you are about to do with these men. For before these days Theudas rose up, claiming to be somebody, and a number of men, about four hundred, joined him. He was killed, and all who followed him were dispersed and came to nothing. After him Judas the Galilean rose up in the days of the census and drew away some of the people after him. He too perished, and all who followed him were scattered. So in the present case I tell you, keep away from these men and let them alone, for if this plan or this undertaking is of man, it will fail; but if it is of God, you will not be able to overthrow them. You might even be found opposing God!" So they took his advice, and when they had called in the apostles, they beat them and charged them not to speak in the name of Jesus, and let them go. Then they left the presence of the council, rejoicing that they were counted worthy to suffer dishonor for the name. And every day, in the temple and from house to house, they did not cease teaching and preaching that the Christ is Jesus.

The Gospel Begins to Spread to the Gentiles

The church in Jerusalem grew quickly from 120 to 3,000 to 5,000 people. The gospel spread outward from Jerusalem to the surrounding areas. But God's plan all along—just as he had promised Abraham—was to bless all nations through Israel. Now that many Israelites were trusting in their Savior, it was time for this largely Jewish church to spread the gospel outward. It was time for the gospel to spread to the "ends of the earth" (Acts 13:47), to every people group on the planet.

This next reading shows how Paul (who was also known by his Hebrew name, Saul) became a Christian. Paul's conversion shows us that no one is too sinful to become a Christian. Paul used to hate and harm Christians, but Jesus loved him and forgave him. Not only that, but Jesus sent Paul to go to the nations to share the good news about him.

B ut Saul, still breathing threats and murder against the disciples of the Lord, went to the high priest and asked him for letters to the synagogues at Damascus, so that if he found any belonging to the Way, men or women, he might bring them bound to Jerusalem. Now as he went on his way, he approached Damascus, and suddenly a light from heaven shone around him. And falling to the ground, he heard a voice saying to him, "Saul, Saul, why are you persecuting me?" And he said, "Who are you, Lord?" And he said, "I am Jesus, whom you are persecuting. But rise and enter the city, and you will be told what you are to do." The men who were traveling with him stood speechless, hearing the voice but seeing no one. Saul rose from the ground, and although his eyes were opened, he saw nothing. So they led him by the hand and brought him into Damascus. And for three days he was without sight, and neither ate nor drank.

Now there was a disciple at Damascus named Ananias. The Lord said to him in a vision, "Ananias." And he said, "Here I am, Lord." And the Lord said to him, "Rise and go to the street called Straight, and at the house of Judas look for a man of Tarsus named Saul, for behold, he is praying, and he has seen in a vision a man named Ananias come in and lay his hands on him so that he might regain his sight." But Ananias answered, "Lord, I have heard from many about this man, how much evil he has done to your saints at Jerusalem. And here he has authority from the chief priests to bind all who call on your name." But the Lord said to him, "Go, for he is a chosen instrument of mine to carry my name before the Gentiles and kings and the children of Israel. For I will show him how much he must suffer for the sake of my name." So Ananias departed and entered the house. And laying his hands on him he said, "Brother Saul, the Lord Jesus who appeared to you on the road by which you came has sent me so that you may regain your sight and be filled with the Holy Spirit." And immediately something like scales fell from his eyes, and he regained his sight. Then he rose and was baptized; and taking food, he was strengthened.

For some days he was with the disciples at Damascus. And immediately he proclaimed Jesus in the synagogues, saying, "He is the Son of God." And all who heard him were amazed and said, "Is not this the man who made havoc in Jerusalem of those who called upon this name? And has he not come here for this purpose, to bring them bound before the chief priests?" But Saul increased all the more in strength, and confounded the Jews who lived in Damascus by proving that Jesus was the Christ.

When many days had passed, the Jews plotted to kill him, but their plot became known to Saul. They were watching the gates day and night in order to kill him, but his disciples took him by night and let him down through an opening in the wall, lowering him in a basket.

And when he had come to Jerusalem, he attempted to join the disciples. And they were all afraid of him, for they did not believe that he was a disciple. But Barnabas took him and brought him to the apostles and declared to them how on the road he had seen the Lord, who spoke to him, and how at Damascus he had preached boldly in the name of Jesus. So he went in and out among them at Jerusalem, preaching boldly in the name of the Lord. And he spoke and disputed against the Hellenists. But they were seeking to kill him. And when the brothers learned this, they brought him down to Caesarea and sent him off to Tarsus.

So the church throughout all Judea and Galilee and Samaria had peace and was being built up. And walking in the fear of the Lord and in the comfort of the Holy Spirit, it multiplied.

The Gospel
Continues to Spread

Paul's conversion shows us the kindness of Jesus' heart. Jesus accepts and saves anyone who comes to him with faith. It does not matter how bad or good he is, how young or old he is, or what color of skin he has. Jesus loved Paul even though Paul did many bad things. Jesus forgave him for all his sins and transformed his heart so that he could love God and others. If there is room in God's kingdom for someone like Paul, there is room in God's kingdom for anyone—even you or me.

The rest of Acts shows how Paul went on several missionary journeys to tell others about Jesus. He spread the gospel and started churches all across modern-day Turkey and parts of Europe. Even though Paul suffered for being a Christian, Jesus kept strengthening him, and he kept trusting Jesus. This next passage shows us the beginning of Paul's journeys.

ACTS 13:1–52

Now there were in the church at Antioch prophets and teachers, Barnabas, Simeon who was called Niger, Lucius of Cyrene, Manaen a lifelong friend of Herod the tetrarch, and Saul. While they were worshiping the Lord and fasting, the Holy Spirit said, "Set apart for me Barnabas and Saul for the work to which I have called them." Then after fasting and praying they laid their hands on them and sent them off.

So, being sent out by the Holy Spirit, they went down to Seleucia, and from there they sailed to Cyprus. When they arrived at Salamis, they proclaimed the word of God in the synagogues of the Jews. And they had John to assist them. When they had gone through the whole island as far as Paphos, they came upon a certain magician, a Jewish false prophet named Bar-Jesus. He was with the proconsul, Sergius Paulus, a man of intelligence, who summoned Barnabas and Saul and sought to hear the word of God. But Elymas the magician (for that is the meaning of his name) opposed them, seeking to turn the proconsul away from the faith. But Saul, who was also called Paul, filled with the Holy Spirit, looked intently at him and said, "You son of the devil, you enemy of all righteousness, full of all deceit and villainy, will you not stop making crooked the straight paths of the Lord? And now, behold, the hand of the Lord is upon you, and you will be blind and unable to see the sun for a time." Immediately mist and darkness fell upon him, and he went about seeking people to lead him by the hand. Then the proconsul believed, when he saw what had occurred, for he was astonished at the teaching of the Lord.

Now Paul and his companions set sail from Paphos and came to Perga in Pamphylia. And John left them and returned to Jerusalem, but they went on from Perga and came to Antioch in Pisidia. And on the Sabbath day they went into the synagogue and sat down. After the reading from the Law and the Prophets, the rulers of the synagogue sent a message to them, saying, "Brothers, if you have any word of encouragement for the people, say it." So Paul stood up, and motioning with his hand said:

"Men of Israel and you who fear God, listen. The God of this people Israel chose our fathers and made the people great during their stay in the land of Egypt, and with uplifted arm he led them out of it. And for about forty years he put up with them in the wilderness. And after destroying seven nations in the land of Canaan, he gave them their land as an inheritance. All this took about 450 years. And after that he gave them judges until Samuel the prophet. Then they asked for a king, and God gave them Saul the son of Kish, a man of the tribe of Benjamin, for forty years. And when he had removed him, he raised up David to be their king, of whom he testified and said, 'I have found in David the son of Jesse a man after my heart, who will do all my will.' Of this man's offspring God has brought to Israel a Savior, Jesus, as he promised. Before his coming, John had proclaimed a baptism of repentance to all the people of Israel. And as John was finishing his course, he said, 'What do you suppose that I am? I am not he. No, but behold, after me one is coming, the sandals of whose feet I am not worthy to untie.'

"Brothers, sons of the family of Abraham, and those among you who fear God, to us has been sent the message of this salvation. For those who live in Jerusalem and their rulers, because they did not recognize him nor understand the utterances of the prophets, which are read every Sabbath, fulfilled them by condemning him. And though they found in him no guilt worthy of death, they asked Pilate to have him executed. And when they had carried out all that was written of him, they took him down from the tree and laid him in a tomb. But God raised him from the dead, and for many days he appeared to those who had come up with him from Galilee to Jerusalem, who are now his witnesses to the people. And we bring you the good news that what God promised to the fathers, this he has fulfilled to us their children by raising Jesus, as also it is written in the second Psalm,

> "'You are my Son,
>> today I have begotten you.'

And as for the fact that he raised him from the dead, no more to return to corruption, he has spoken in this way,

> "'I will give you the holy and sure blessings of David.'

Therefore he says also in another psalm,

> "'You will not let your Holy One see corruption.'

For David, after he had served the purpose of God in his own generation, fell asleep and was laid with his fathers and saw corruption, but he whom God raised up did not see corruption. Let it be known to you therefore, brothers, that through this man forgiveness of sins is proclaimed to you, and by him everyone who believes is freed from everything from which you could not be freed by the law of Moses. Beware, therefore, lest what is said in the Prophets should come about:

> "'Look, you scoffers,
>> be astounded and perish;
>> for I am doing a work in your days,
>>> a work that you will not believe, even if one tells it
>>>> to you.'"

As they went out, the people begged that these things might be told them the next Sabbath. And after the meeting of the synagogue broke up, many Jews and devout converts to Judaism followed Paul and Barnabas, who, as they spoke with them, urged them to continue in the grace of God.

The next Sabbath almost the whole city gathered to hear the word of the Lord. But when the Jews saw the crowds, they were filled with jealousy and began to contradict what was spoken by Paul, reviling him. And Paul and Barnabas spoke out boldly, saying, "It was necessary that the word of God be spoken first to you. Since you thrust it aside and judge yourselves unworthy of eternal life, behold, we are turning to the Gentiles. For so the Lord has commanded us, saying,

> "'I have made you a light for the Gentiles,
>   that you may bring salvation to the ends of the
>   earth.'"

And when the Gentiles heard this, they began rejoicing and glorifying the word of the Lord, and as many as were appointed to eternal life believed. And the word of the Lord was spreading throughout the whole region. But the Jews incited the devout women of high standing and the leading men of the city, stirred up persecution against Paul and Barnabas, and drove them out of their district. But they shook off the dust from their feet against them and went to Iconium. And the disciples were filled with joy and with the Holy Spirit.

The Gospel Explained

The Gospel of Mark showed us how the kingdom of God arrived through Jesus' life, death, and resurrection. The book of Acts showed us how God's people spread the good news of King Jesus, made disciples, and planted churches. And now letters like Ephesians encourage believers to know Jesus and live all of life as members of his kingdom.

This first part of Ephesians celebrates the blessings of salvation. It shows how each person of the Trinity has an important part in blessing us. The triune God—Father, Son, and Holy Spirit—is like a fountain that overflows with kindness to us. He has a gracious plan to bring everything in the world under the kingship of Jesus. He saves us by grace alone, through faith alone, in Jesus alone—all for our good and his glory.

EPHESIANS 1:1–2:10

Paul, an apostle of Christ Jesus by the will of God,

To the saints who are in Ephesus, and are faithful in Christ Jesus:

Grace to you and peace from God our Father and the Lord Jesus Christ.

Blessed be the God and Father of our Lord Jesus Christ, who has blessed us in Christ with every spiritual blessing in the heavenly places, even as he chose us in him before the foundation of the world, that we should be holy and blameless before him. In love he predestined us for adoption to himself as sons through Jesus Christ, according to the purpose of his will, to the praise of his glorious grace, with which he has blessed us in the Beloved. In him we have redemption through his blood, the forgiveness of our trespasses, according to the riches of his grace, which he lavished upon us, in all wisdom and insight making known to us the mystery of his will, according to his purpose, which he set forth in Christ as a plan for the fullness of time, to unite all things in him, things in heaven and things on earth.

In him we have obtained an inheritance, having been predestined according to the purpose of him who works all things according to the counsel of his will, so that we who were the first to hope in Christ might be to the praise of his glory. In him you also, when you heard the word of truth, the gospel of your salvation, and believed in him, were sealed with the promised Holy Spirit, who is the guarantee of our inheritance until we acquire possession of it, to the praise of his glory.

For this reason, because I have heard of your faith in the Lord Jesus and your love toward all the saints, I do not cease to give thanks for you, remembering you in my prayers, that the God of our Lord Jesus Christ, the Father of glory, may give you the Spirit of wisdom and of revelation in the knowledge of him, having the eyes of your hearts enlightened, that you may know what is the hope to which he has called you, what are the riches of his glorious inheritance in the saints, and what is the immeasurable greatness of his power toward us who believe, according to the working of his great might that he worked in Christ when he raised him from the dead and seated him at his right hand in the heavenly places, far above all rule and authority and power and dominion, and above every name that is named, not only in this age but also in the one to come. And he put all things under his feet and gave him as head over all things to the church, which is his body, the fullness of him who fills all in all.

And you were dead in the trespasses and sins in which you once walked, following the course of this world, following the prince of the power of the air, the spirit that is now at work in the sons of disobedience—among whom we all once lived in the passions of our flesh, carrying out the desires of the body and the mind, and were by nature children of wrath, like the rest of mankind. But God, being rich in mercy, because of the great love with which he loved us, even when we were dead in our trespasses, made us alive together with Christ—by grace you have been saved—and raised us up with him and seated us with him in the heavenly places in Christ Jesus, so that in the coming ages he might show the immeasurable riches of his grace in kindness toward us in Christ Jesus. For by grace you have been saved through faith. And this is not your own doing; it is the gift of God, not a result of works, so that no one may boast. For we are his workmanship, created in Christ Jesus for good works, which God prepared beforehand, that we should walk in them.

The Gospel Applied

The first part of Ephesians celebrated the blessings God gives to Christians. Those who trust Jesus have been chosen, adopted, forgiven, and made spiritually alive in Christ. And all this comes to us not because *we* are good but because *he* is good.

This next part of Ephesians shows what difference this makes in our lives. The wonderful truth about the gospel leads us to live a new kind of life. As we continue to know and trust in Jesus, we become transformed to be more like him! The Holy Spirit begins to make us humble, gentle, and patient with other people. We start to think and feel and speak and act more like Jesus — more like the kind of person God made us to be. We do not do this in order to get blessings from God; we do it because he has already given us everything we need.

EPHESIANS 4:1-32

I therefore, a prisoner for the Lord, urge you to walk in a manner worthy of the calling to which you have been called, with all humility and gentleness, with patience, bearing with one another in love, eager to maintain the unity of the Spirit in the bond of peace. There is one body and one Spirit—just as you were called to the one hope that belongs to your call—one Lord, one faith, one baptism, one God and Father of all, who is over all and through all and in all. But grace was given to each one of us according to the measure of Christ's gift. Therefore it says,

"When he ascended on high he led a host of captives,
and he gave gifts to men."

(In saying, "He ascended," what does it mean but that he had also descended into the lower regions, the earth? He who descended is the one who also ascended far above all the heavens, that he might fill all things.) And he gave the apostles, the prophets, the evangelists, the shepherds and teachers, to equip the saints for the work of ministry, for building up the body of Christ, until we all attain to the unity of the faith and of the knowledge of the Son of God, to mature manhood, to the measure of the stature of the fullness of Christ, so that we may no longer be children, tossed to and fro by the waves and carried about by every wind of doctrine, by human cunning, by craftiness in deceitful schemes. Rather, speaking the truth in love, we are to grow up in every way into him who is the head, into Christ, from whom the whole body, joined and held together by every joint with which it is equipped, when each part is working properly, makes the body grow so that it builds itself up in love.

Now this I say and testify in the Lord, that you must no longer walk as the Gentiles do, in the futility of their minds. They are darkened in their understanding, alienated from the life of God because of the ignorance that is in them, due to their hardness of heart. They have become callous and have given themselves up to sensuality, greedy to practice every kind of impurity. But that is not the way you learned Christ!—assuming that you have heard about him and were taught in him, as the truth is in Jesus, to put off your old self, which belongs to your former manner of life and is corrupt through deceitful desires, and to be renewed in the spirit of your minds, and to put on the new self, created after the likeness of God in true righteousness and holiness.

Therefore, having put away falsehood, let each one of you speak the truth with his neighbor, for we are members one of another. Be angry and do not sin; do not let the sun go down on your anger, and give no opportunity to the devil. Let the thief no longer steal, but rather let him labor, doing honest work with his own hands, so that he may have something to share with anyone in need. Let no corrupting talk come out of your mouths, but only such as is good for building up, as fits the occasion, that it may give grace to those who hear. And do not grieve the Holy Spirit of God, by whom you were sealed for the day of redemption. Let all bitterness and wrath and anger and clamor and slander be put away from you, along with all malice. Be kind to one another, tenderhearted, forgiving one another, as God in Christ forgave you.

The King Speaks
to His Churches

Ever since sin entered the world, God began to unfold his plan of grace. He promised to send a Savior who would renew people and all creation. Jesus has now come to do this. In his death he took our death. In his resurrection he brought us life. And when he returns, he will make all things new.

As those who trust Jesus and wait for him, we have a mission. We are to multiply by making more disciples and churches. But what should our lives and churches look like? This next reading shows us. The apostle John received this symbolic vision that reveals to us that Jesus is our King, that he is with his churches, and that he has a message for us. As he speaks to his churches, he encourages them and calls them to faithfulness.

REVELATION 1:9–2:11

I, John, your brother and partner in the tribulation and the kingdom and the patient endurance that are in Jesus, was on the island called Patmos on account of the word of God and the testimony of Jesus. I was in the Spirit on the Lord's day, and I heard behind me a loud voice like a trumpet saying, "Write what you see in a book and send it to the seven churches, to Ephesus and to Smyrna and to Pergamum and to Thyatira and to Sardis and to Philadelphia and to Laodicea."

Then I turned to see the voice that was speaking to me, and on turning I saw seven golden lampstands, and in the midst of the lampstands one like a son of man, clothed with a long robe and with a golden sash around his chest. The hairs of his head were white, like white wool, like snow. His eyes were like a flame of fire, his feet were like burnished bronze, refined in a furnace, and his voice was like the roar of many waters. In his right hand he held seven stars, from his mouth came a sharp two-edged sword, and his face was like the sun shining in full strength.

When I saw him, I fell at his feet as though dead. But he laid his right hand on me, saying, "Fear not, I am the first and the last, and the living one. I died, and behold I am alive forevermore, and I have the keys of Death and Hades. Write therefore the things that you have seen, those that are and those that are to take place after this. As for the mystery of the seven stars that you saw in my right hand, and the seven golden lampstands, the seven stars are the angels of the seven churches, and the seven lampstands are the seven churches.

"To the angel of the church in Ephesus write: 'The words of him who holds the seven stars in his right hand, who walks among the seven golden lampstands.

"'I know your works, your toil and your patient endurance, and how you cannot bear with those who are evil, but have tested those who call themselves apostles and are not, and found them to be false. I know you are enduring patiently and bearing up for my name's sake, and you have not grown weary. But I have this against you, that you have abandoned the love you had at first. Remember therefore from where you have fallen; repent, and do the works you did at first. If not, I will come to you and remove your lampstand from its place, unless you repent. Yet this you have: you hate the works of the Nicolaitans, which I also hate. He who has an ear, let him hear what the Spirit says to the churches. To the one who conquers I will grant to eat of the tree of life, which is in the paradise of God.'

"And to the angel of the church in Smyrna write: 'The words of the first and the last, who died and came to life.

"'I know your tribulation and your poverty (but you are rich) and the slander of those who say that they are Jews and are not, but are a synagogue of Satan. Do not fear what you are about to suffer. Behold, the devil is about to throw some of you into prison, that you may be tested, and for ten days you will have tribulation. Be faithful unto death, and I will give you the crown of life. He who has an ear, let him hear what the Spirit says to the churches. The one who conquers will not be hurt by the second death.' "

The Return of the King
and the Restoration
of All Things

God made and blessed us. But we walked away from him. Yet now he is unfolding his plan of grace to bring us back again. He promised to send a Savior who would defeat evil, restore people to himself, and ultimately renew the whole creation. Jesus has come to do all this. He lived a perfect life of trust and obedience to the Father. He died in our place and rose again to bring forgiveness and to restore our relationship with him. He sent his Spirit to change our hearts and bring healing to relationships. And he will come again to raise all his people from the dead to live in a new creation with him forever. It will be like Eden again—but better, just as this final chapter of the Bible describes.

Yet this reading also teaches that there are two paths. One path is for those who reject God and will endure eternal punishment and death. The other path is for all who trust God's mercy in Christ. These will enjoy true friendship with God and his people in a new creation forever. There will be no more sin, no more death, and no more crying. Instead, we will enjoy God's kindness to us in Jesus forever.

REVELATION 21:1–8

Then I saw a new heaven and a new earth, for the first heaven and the first earth had passed away, and the sea was no more. And I saw the holy city, new Jerusalem, coming down out of heaven from God, prepared as a bride adorned for her husband. And I heard a loud voice from the throne saying, "Behold, the dwelling place of God is with man. He will dwell with them, and they will be his people, and God himself will be with them as their God. He will wipe away every tear from their eyes, and death shall be no more, neither shall there be mourning, nor crying, nor pain anymore, for the former things have passed away."

And he who was seated on the throne said, "Behold, I am making all things new." Also he said, "Write this down, for these words are trustworthy and true." And he said to me, "It is done! I am the Alpha and the Omega, the beginning and the end. To the thirsty I will give from the spring of the water of life without payment. The one who conquers will have this heritage, and I will be his God and he will be my son. But as for the cowardly, the faithless, the detestable, as for murderers, the sexually immoral, sorcerers, idolaters, and all liars, their portion will be in the lake that burns with fire and sulfur, which is the second death."

REVELATION 22:1–21

Then the angel showed me the river of the water of life, bright as crystal, flowing from the throne of God and of the Lamb through the middle of the street of the city; also, on either side of the river, the tree of life with its twelve kinds of fruit, yielding its fruit each month. The leaves of the tree were for the healing of the nations. No longer will there be anything accursed, but the throne of God and of the Lamb will be in it, and his servants will worship him. They will see his face, and his name will be on their foreheads. And night will be no more. They will need no light of lamp or sun, for the Lord God will be their light, and they will reign forever and ever.

And he said to me, "These words are trustworthy and true. And the Lord, the God of the spirits of the prophets, has sent his angel to show his servants what must soon take place."

"And behold, I am coming soon. Blessed is the one who keeps the words of the prophecy of this book."

I, John, am the one who heard and saw these things. And when I heard and saw them, I fell down to worship at the feet of the angel who showed them to me, but he said to me, "You must not do that! I am a fellow servant with you and your brothers the prophets, and with those who keep the words of this book. Worship God."

And he said to me, "Do not seal up the words of the prophecy of this book, for the time is near. Let the evildoer still do evil, and the filthy still be filthy, and the righteous still do right, and the holy still be holy."

"Behold, I am coming soon, bringing my recompense with me, to repay each one for what he has done. I am the Alpha and the Omega, the first and the last, the beginning and the end."

Blessed are those who wash their robes, so that they may have the right to the tree of life and that they may enter the city by the gates. Outside are the dogs and sorcerers and the sexually immoral and murderers and idolaters, and everyone who loves and practices falsehood.

"I, Jesus, have sent my angel to testify to you about these things for the churches. I am the root and the descendant of David, the bright morning star."

The Spirit and the Bride say, "Come." And let the one who hears say, "Come." And let the one who is thirsty come; let the one who desires take the water of life without price.

I warn everyone who hears the words of the prophecy of this book: if anyone adds to them, God will add to him the plagues described in this book, and if anyone takes away from the words of the book of this prophecy, God will take away his share in the tree of life and in the holy city, which are described in this book.

He who testifies to these things says, "Surely I am coming soon." Amen. Come, Lord Jesus!

The grace of the Lord Jesus be with all. Amen.

COLOPHON

Typeset and designed by Crossway.

Introductions by Drew Hunter.

Illustrations by Peter Voth.